Youth Basketball Drills

Burrall Paye

Patrick Paye

Human Kinetics

Library of Congress Cataloging-in-Publication Data

Paye, Burrall, 1938-
    Youth basketball drills / Burrall Paye, Patrick Paye.
       p.   cm.
    ISBN 0-7360-3365-3
      1. Youth league basketball--Coaching.   I. Paye, Patrick, 1965-   II. Title.
   GV886.3 .P39   2001
   796.323'07'7--dc21   00-056724

ISBN: 0-7360-3365-3

Managing Editor: Leigh LaHood
Proofreader: Bob Replinger
Graphic Designer: Fred Starbird
Graphic Artist: Sandra Meier
Cover Designer: Keith Blomberg
Photographer (cover and interior): Tom Roberts
Illustrator: Figures on pages 9 and 155-157 by Tom Roberts; all other figures by Sharon Smith
Printer: Bang Printing

Human Kinetics books are available at special discounts for bulk purchase. Special editions or book excerpts can also be created to specification. For details, contact the Special Sales Manager at Human Kinetics.

Printed in the United States of America   10 9 8 7 6 5 4 3

Human Kinetics
Web site: www.HumanKinetics.com

United States: Human Kinetics, P.O. Box 5076, Champaign, IL 61825-5076
800-747-4457
e-mail: humank@hkusa.com

Canada: Human Kinetics, 475 Devonshire Road, Unit 100, Windsor, ON N8Y 2L5
800-465-7301 (in Canada only)
e-mail: orders@hkcanada.com

Europe: Human Kinetics, 107 Bradford Road, Stanningley
Leeds LS28 6AT, United Kingdom
+44 (0) 113 255 5665
e-mail: hk@hkeurope.com

Australia: Human Kinetics, 57A Price Avenue, Lower Mitcham, South Australia 5062
08 8277 1555
e-mail: liahka@senet.com.au

New Zealand: Human Kinetics, P.O. Box 105-231, Auckland Central
09-523-3462
e-mail: hkp@ihug.co.nz

To my dear wife, Nancy,
my associate coach for nearly 40 years
and still counting.

Burrall

To Mom, Dad, and Michele.
Thanks.

Patrick

Contents

PART **I** OFFENSIVE SKILLS AND DRILLS

PART **II** **DEFENSIVE SKILLS AND DRILLS**

Drill Finder

Drill no.	Drill title	Time (min)	# of players		Skill level			Page no.
			Team	Indiv.	Begin.	Inter.	Advan.	
1	Running Outside the Line	3	✓	✓	✓	✓	✓	4
2	Mirror Slap	2	✓		✓	✓	✓	7
3	Dribbling off the Wall	1		✓	✓	✓	✓	8
4	Lane Slide	1	✓	✓	✓	✓	✓	10
5	Basic Layup	3	✓		✓	✓	✓	14
6	Triple-Threat Position	2	✓	✓	✓	✓	✓	16
7	Post Position	5	✓	✓	✓	✓	✓	18
8	Rocker Step	5		✓	✓			20
9	In-and-Out Move	5		✓	✓			22
10	Crossover Move	5		✓	✓			24
11	Spin (Reverse) Move	5		✓	✓			26
12	Half-Spin Move	5		✓	✓			28
13	Combination Dribbling Moves	3		✓			✓	30
14	Fingertip Drill	30 sec		✓	✓	✓		35
15	Standing Figure 8	2	✓	✓	✓	✓		36
16	Figure 8 Dribble	2	✓	✓	✓	✓	✓	38
17	Side-to-Side Dribble	2	✓	✓	✓	✓	✓	40
18	Spider Dribble	30 sec	✓	✓	✓			41
19	Speed Dribble	1	✓	✓	✓		✓	42
20	Control Dribble	1	✓	✓	✓		✓	44
21	Change of Pace	1	✓	✓	✓		✓	46
22	Hesitation Dribble	1	✓	✓		✓	✓	48
23	Retreating Dribble	1	✓	✓		✓	✓	50

Drill no.	Drill title	Time (min)	# of players		Skill level			Page no.
			Team	Indiv.	Begin.	Inter.	Advan.	
24	In-and-Out Dribble Maneuver	1	✓	✓		✓	✓	52
25	Crossover Dribble Maneuver	1	✓	✓		✓	✓	54
26	Spin (Reverse) Dribble Maneuver	1	✓	✓		✓	✓	56
27	Half-Spin Dribble Maneuver	1	✓	✓		✓	✓	58
28	Fun Cone Dribbling Drill	2	✓	✓	✓	✓		60
29	Dribble Tag	1	✓	✓	✓	✓		62
30	Team Dribble Tag	1	✓	✓	✓			64
31	Front Pivot	2	✓	✓	✓	✓		68
32	Reverse Pivot	2	✓	✓	✓	✓		70
33	Jump Stop	1	✓	✓	✓	✓	✓	72
34	Stride Stop (One-Two)	1	✓	✓	✓	✓	✓	74
35	One-on-Two Pivoting	$1\frac{1}{2}$	✓	✓	✓	✓		76
36	Dribble, Stop, Pivot	1	✓	✓	✓	✓		78
37	Dribble, Stop, Pivot, Pass, Cut	3	✓			✓	✓	80
38	Two-Line Standing Still Drill	3	✓		✓	✓	✓	84
39	Two-Line Moving Drill	3	✓		✓	✓	✓	86
40	Two-Line Fullcourt Passing Drill	2	✓			✓		88
41	Two-on-One Passing Drill	$1\frac{1}{2}$	✓			✓		90
42	Pepper Passing Drill	2	✓		✓		✓	92
43	Three-on-Three Trapping and Passing Drill	3	✓			✓	✓	94
44	Passing, Dribbling, Trapping Drill	10	✓				✓	96
45	Four-Corner Passing Drill	3	✓		✓	✓	✓	98
46	Touch Passing and Layup Drill	3	✓			✓		100

(continued)

Drill no.	Drill title	Time (min)	# of players		Skill level			Page no.
			Team	Indiv.	Begin.	Inter.	Advan.	
47	V-Cut	3	✓	✓	✓	✓	✓	104
48	Middle Cut	3	✓	✓	✓	✓	✓	106
49	Back-Door Cut	3	✓	✓	✓	✓	✓	108
50	Flash Pivot Cutting	3	✓	✓	✓	✓		110
51	Flash Pivot, Triple Threat, and Offensive Moves	10	✓	✓	✓	✓	✓	112
52	Two-Player Cutting Drill	3	✓		✓			114
53	Three-Player Cutting Drill	9	✓		✓			116
54	Two-on-Two Pass, Dribble, and Cut	3	✓		✓			120
55	Two-on-Two Recognition	6	✓			✓	✓	122
56	Three-on-Three Passing, Cutting, and Spacing	4	✓			✓		124
57	Three-on-Three Passing, Cutting, Dribbling, Spacing	6	✓			✓		126
58	Three-on-Three Pass, Cut, and Recognition	6	✓			✓	✓	128
59	Pass and Screen Away	10	✓	✓	✓	✓	✓	132
60	Pass and Screen on the Ball	6	✓	✓		✓		134
61	Three-Player Screening Drill	4	✓		✓			136
62	Three-on-Three Pass, Screen, and Recognition	4	✓			✓	✓	138
63	Tip the Ball off the Wall and Pivot	1		✓	✓		✓	142
64	Bull in the Ring	4	✓	✓	✓	✓	✓	144
65	Jab Step and Roll	2	✓	✓		✓	✓	146
66	Wave Bye	1	✓	✓	✓			150
67	Form Flip-Ball Drill	1	✓	✓	✓			151

Drill no.	Drill title	Time (min)	# of players		Skill level			Page no.
			Team	Indiv.	Begin.	Inter.	Advan.	
68	Lift, Extend, Flip	1	✓	✓	✓	✓		152
69	Lying Down Flip-Ball Drill	1	✓	✓	✓	✓		154
70	Flip the Ball off the Wall	1		✓	✓	✓		155
71	Around the World	10	✓	✓	✓	✓	✓	158
72	No Rim Drill	10	✓	✓	✓		✓	160
73	21	6	✓		✓			162
74	NBA Shooting Drill	2		✓	✓			163
75	Post-Up Mechanics	5	✓	✓			✓	166
76	Slide Step Dribble	1	✓	✓	✓		✓	168
77	Fronting	2	✓	✓		✓		170
78	Two-Step Drill	5	✓	✓		✓		172
79	Roll Step	5	✓	✓			✓	174
80	Three-Quarter Drill	5	✓	✓		✓		176
81	High-Low Post Passing	6	✓			✓	✓	178
82	Post Screening	10	✓			✓	✓	180
83	One-on-One Lane Drill	4		✓	✓			184
84	One-on-One Relief Drill	4		✓	✓			186
85	One-on-One Team Drill	2		✓	✓			188
86	One on One on One on One	4	✓		✓			190
87	One-on-One Fullcourt Game	5	✓	✓	✓			192
88	Recovery Drill	6	✓	✓	✓			194
89	Approach and Close Out	6	✓	✓	✓			196
90	On Ball: Screen and Roll, Screen and Fade, Pass and Blast	10	✓			✓	✓	198
91	Away From Ball: Screen and Replace or Replace Yourself	10	✓			✓		200

(continued)

Drill no.	Drill title	Time (min)	# of players		Skill level			Page no.
			Team	Indiv.	Begin.	Inter.	Advan.	
92	Three-on-Three No-Dribble Drill	5	✓		✓			202
93	Three-on-Three Name Move	6	✓		✓			204
94	Follow the Rules	9	✓			✓	✓	206
95	Five-on-Five With No Defense	6	✓		✓		✓	208
96	Fence Slide	1	✓	✓	✓	✓	✓	214
97	Front Foot to Pivot Foot	3	✓	✓		✓		216
98	Interception Stance	3	✓	✓	✓	✓		218
99	Defensive Step Drill	1		✓	✓			222
100	Overplay Step Drill	2		✓	✓			224
101	Mirror Step Drill	2	✓	✓	✓			226
102	Mass Wave Sliding Drill	1	✓	✓	✓			230
103	Jump to the Ball	5	✓		✓			232
104	Deny the Wing	4	✓		✓	✓		234
105	Deny the Flash Pivot	4	✓		✓	✓		236
106	Dribbler Closeout	1	✓	✓	✓	✓	✓	238
107	Skip Pass and Closeout	6	✓			✓		240
108	Eight-Point Drill	10	✓	✓			✓	242
109	Shell Drill	10	✓				✓	246
110	Five-on-Five		✓		✓			248

Introduction

Youngsters ages 6 to 14, male or female, who want to become super basketball players will find the tools they need in this book. Athletes may practice many of the drills in this book (marked "Individual") by themselves. For the improvement to begin, all a player needs are a basketball, a goal, and this book.

Coaches will find here everything necessary to develop outstanding players—which translates into win after win after win. While winning comes from the player's development, the coach's greatest pleasure will come from seeing protégés' dribbling improve, moves unfold, stances and slides emerge, passing skills evolve, and shooting talents grow. There is no fulfillment like it. This book includes a section on how to practice, as well as how to create a practice schedule. Absolutely no prior experience is required.

Parents want their children to learn the fundamentals correctly. By working closely with the youngsters in developing athletic skills, parents and children form solid bonds much like those that develop among teammates of ballclubs.

Each drill, when practiced correctly and perfected, leads to an advanced basketball basic. And once the muscle memorizes that rudiment, it becomes as intrinsic as riding a bicycle: the athlete's muscle never forgets it. The key is to perform the fundamental correctly at first and not have to relearn it at a later date.

How This Book Will Help You

This book offers unlimited opportunities to perfect one's game. Each drill is presented in a format intended to teach only one specific technique until it is learned. Most drills begin with an individual basic fundamental. Then many drill sections follow with an intermediate and an advanced skill development drill. These are progressive, aimed at developing skill levels from the biddy league to the collegiate level.

It is very important that the player execute each fundamental exactly as stated in the drill. This proper execution eliminates the necessity of relearning the rudiment. Once the skill is learned correctly, the player should quicken up the delivery. It is the quick, explosive first steps that are all-important in basketball. Don't execute fast; do perform quickly. Speed is often a detriment. So learn correctly, then make the move quicker and quicker and quicker, until it is explosively quick; but do not make the move faster.

For example, in the section on shooting, the athlete will find that the beginning drill simply shows him how to put the ball in his hand properly. Next comes learning how to flip the ball. Then proper lifting and extending the arm. Then a drill to keep the elbow in—the crooked elbow is the worst fault in all of basketball and is almost uncorrectable once the muscle has memorized it incorrectly. After that, the player develops a follow-through with a simple "waving goodbye" drill. Put it all together, and the athlete has a picture-perfect shot. All that remains is to practice getting the shot off more quickly without rushing it.

Coaches will find that each drill teaches another phase of basketball. The progressiveness of each drill's mechanical movement allows you to teach even the youngest member of your squad the basics, and to teach them correctly. Too often the youngster learns poor techniques early, and it is almost impossible to correct those mannerisms as the young player grows older.

You will also find that as you teach the drills, the student is not only learning basic fundamentals of basketball, but also is understanding a system of play. The squad will become proficient at moving with the basketball, cutting without the basketball, and understanding the strategies of the game. At the end of the drilling, you will find your team can play the motion offense, the most widely used offensive system in high schools, colleges, and the professional leagues. Your team members will also know how to play man-to-man defense.

You do not have to know basketball to teach these things to your protégés. All the little details are given with each drill, under the section called Teaching Points. And each drill is broken down to different levels: beginner, intermediate, and advanced.

Each drill also refers you to related drills. This enables you to continue teaching the same rudiment while adding the next step in development, keeping staleness away from your practice sessions. You can teach the same rudiments using different drills, keeping freshness in the steps of your protégés.

As the season progresses, you will discover that this arrangement of the book makes it a perfect reference tool. You have the dual pleasure of watching your athlete grow and mature correctly while also learning the most-used offense (motion) and defense (man-to-man) in all of basketball. Other coaches will be envious of you.

The youngster's parents want the best for their child. They want them to learn techniques, movements, and footwork correctly. Too often young children drill incorrectly, and their muscles memorize incorrect movements. This prevents young athletes from progressing to their highest potential talent level. This book removes that obstacle. When the youngster starts out executing each move, each technique, each rudiment exactly as it was meant to be developed, the improvement never stops until the muscular makeup of the youngster reaches its zenith.

As high school coaches, we have seen so many potentially good athletes have to step aside as they try to advance to higher levels of competition because their muscles have memorized incorrect techniques, like the crooked elbow in shooting. Their successful shots, for example, would never reach an acceptable percentage. All this because they learned the fundamental incorrectly in the beginning. And it is so very difficult to correct those ingrained memories in their muscles. By doing it incorrectly in the beginning, the child stopped progressing.

By following the instructions and illustrations in this book, the child will see exactly how to perform a particular basketball feat. The youngster can even take this book outside to the neighborhood goal and follow the sequence until the technique is learned properly.

About the Drills

This book is made up of 110 drills. Each drill starts with the simplest and goes to the more complex. Each is clearly marked by number and by name. Each indicates whether it is for individuals, teams, or individuals and teams.

Every drill starts with a section called Skill Focus. You will know immediately whether you want to work on this drill today or leave it for another day, because each fundamental to be drilled is listed. Numbers in parentheses show which drills contain an explanation of how to teach that basic skill.

At the top of each drill we indicate how much time it takes to execute the drill with 10 players and 2 coaches. Should your squad consist of more players or fewer coaches, you will need to make time adjustments. The time needed to run a drill is also listed in the drill finder; this can be used as a reference tool when you are making out your practice schedule.

Next we give the procedures, which explain how to do the drill. You need to follow the numbered guidelines step by step. Progressions are offered in almost all the drills. The progression sequence will always be clearly marked—Beginner, Intermediate, or Advanced. The youngest-level sandlot coach may initially want to use only the beginner drills, then progress to the intermediate level as the skills of the individual players improve. The older player's youth coach could probably use the entire spectrum of drills, especially if the sandlot coaches had previously used this book. The high school coach may use the complete scope of drills, based solely on the needs of the moment.

Variations, or options, of the drill are presented under the procedures for each skill level. This will allow you to choose a slightly different setup to accomplish the same fundamental or a slightly more advanced basic.

Teaching Points comprise another component of each drill. This segment tells all the little details you need to know to teach the basketball aspects of that single drill. The teaching points are presented in a form that requires no previous knowledge of the techniques of basketball. If teaching points are not listed in a drill, there are no new basketball basics for the drill except those listed in the Skill Focus section.

Lastly, we list all related drills. This enables you to build a practice plan of perfect order. The second skill to be learned is derived from the first, and on and on and on. You can use one drill to teach the mechanics and use a related drill for fun. You can change your drills and still teach the same fundamentals. Just go to a related drill.

Almost every drill has a diagram or illustration to help you teach the rudiment even if you have never seen a basketball game or practice. Simplicity is one of the keys to fully learning any skill.

And once you are finished with all the drills, you will be running the motion offense and man-to-man defense. And you will be executing those team concepts using accurate and errorless techniques, fundamentals, foot movement, strategy, and methodology. Your kids will grow and grow and grow and GROW.

Let's go drill.

Key to Diagrams

⟶	Player movement without the ball
⇢	Pass or shot
∿∿∿⟶	Dribble
⟶⊣	Screen
①, ②	Offensive player
X1, X2	Defensive player
R	Rebound
Coach	Coach
⚘	Cone

PART

I

. . . .

OFFENSIVE
SKILLS AND DRILLS

CHAPTER 1

Balance, Quickness, and Agility

Proper balance provides explosive, quick movement. Explosive quickness is the first priority of a great one-on-one player.

What is proper balance? How does one get that balance? There are two types of proper balance. The first type is needed when running fullcourt, when speed is more important than control. You want to have an erect stance with your head directly over your torso, which is leaning slightly forward; a slight bend at the knees; and a longer stride, landing on your toes on each stride.

Second, *control balance* requires a shorter step and more bend at the knees (no more than a 135-degree angle). Your head should again be directly over your torso, and your torso should be bent slightly but your back straight and not humped; your toes should be grabbing at the floor, and you want to land heel-toe.

Quickness comes from proper balance. It requires playing on your toes until you get ready to stop; then you want to land your heels first and come up on your toes. Concentration and intensity add to quickness.

Agility is control of your body—and you will need to put your body in all sorts of contortions as you climb the ladder of competition.

Balance, quickness, and agility are developed in the four drills presented in this chapter. Drill 1 requires not only quick movement, but also basketball knowledge. Add other steps to it as you become more skillful and knowledgeable.

Drill 2 compels you to react quickly and explosively, an indispensable skill for one-on-one play. Drill 3 develops maximum agility. Drill 4 accentuates the grabbing of the toes on the floor.

1 Running Outside the Line

Individual or team • 3 minutes

Skill Focus ▶ Quickness, balance, and agility; conditioning; triple-threat position (6); in and out (9, 24); crossover (10, 25); spin (11, 26); half spin (12, 27); front pivot (31); reverse pivot (32); jump stop (33); stride stop (34); slide step (40, 99); V-cut (47); fence slide (96); advance step (99); retreat step (99); swing step (99)

1. Line players up in a straight line at one baseline.
2. Have all players face to the right.
3. On the command "jog," all players begin jogging around the out-of-bounds lines.
4. Have players react to the following verbal commands according to skill level.

Beginner

   a. "Jump stop"—Players stop, using jump stops. "Go"—Players begin jogging again. This continues around the court.

   b. "Stride stop"—Players stop, using stride stops. "Go"—Players begin jogging again.

   c. "Step in"—Players continue jogging but step once into the court, then back on the line. "Step out"—Players continue jogging but step once out of bounds, then back on the line.

   d. "In and out"—Players execute the in-and-out offensive move, then resume jogging.

Intermediate

   a. "Front pivot"—Players use jump stop (or stride stop) and execute a front pivot. Players continue jogging, but now in the opposite direction.

   b. "Reverse pivot"—Players use jump stop (or stride stop) and execute a reverse pivot. Players continue jogging, but now in the opposite direction.

   c. "Jab step"—Players execute a hard jab step with either foot, then continue jogging.

   d. "Crossover step"—Players execute a crossover step with either foot, then continue jogging.

   e. "Spin step"—Players execute a spin step with either foot as the pivot foot, then continue jogging.

   f. "Half-spin step"—Players execute a half-spin step with either foot as the pivot foot, then continue jogging.

a. "Sprint"—Players sprint for five steps, then resume jogging.

b. "V-cut"—Players V-cut, then resume jogging.

c. "Break down"—Players break down into proper defensive stance and remain there, then begin jogging again on "jog."

d. "Pat the floor"—Players break down into defensive stance and pat the floor with their toes as quickly as they can, then resume jogging.

e. "Triple threat"—Players jump stop or stride stop and get into the offensive triple-threat position, then resume jogging.

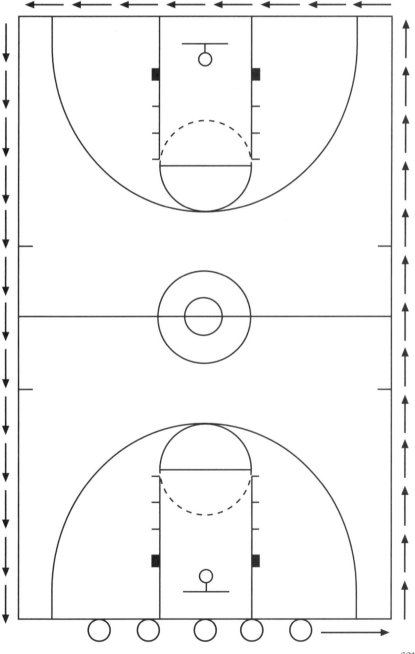

continued

f. "Fence slide"—Players use the defensive fence slide for five steps, then resume jogging.

g. "Advance step"—Players execute a jump stop, then one defensive advance step, then resume jogging.

h. "Retreat step"—Players execute a jump stop, then one defensive retreat step, then resume jogging.

i. "Swing step"—Players execute a jump stop, then one defensive swing step, then resume jogging.

Options ▶
(all skill levels)

1. Instead of just jogging, players must flip a basketball from hand to hand.

2. Instead of just jogging, players must dribble a basketball.

Related Drills: 2, 6, 9-12, 21-27, 31, 32, 47, 50, 51, 54, 65, 83-94, 96, 99

2 Mirror Slap

Team • 2 minutes

Skill Focus ▶ Quickness; stances (4-6); steps (9-12, 24-27, 97-99); defensive fakes (97); pivots (31-32); step-through (35)

Beginner

1. One player lines up facing another; one is player A, and the other is player B. Do this in sets of two all over the court.
2. Player A does a movement and player B tries to mirror it.
3. Instruct players to touch the head with the right hand, then with the left hand, and then with both hands; next, they touch the knee with the right hand, and then with the left hand; finally, players run in place, then pat the floor rapidly with both feet.
4. Player A leads and player B mirrors for 30 seconds or 1 minute. Then player B leads and player A mirrors.
5. In player A, look for precision in performing the techniques; observe how quickly player B reacts.

Intermediate

1. In addition to the quick touches listed for the beginners, intermediate players should show the fakes: jab step, rocker step, in and out, spin, half spin, front pivot, and reverse pivot.

Advanced

1. Advanced players should add defensive stances, fakes, and footwork: interception stance, front foot to pivot foot stance, advance step, retreat step, swing step, slide step, and fence slide, as well as the triple-threat position and the V-cut.
2. Also, have advanced players add the in-and-out defensive fake. To execute, the player steps in with the front foot and strikes the front hand forward quickly (like the strike of a snake), then steps back quickly. This move is used to try to get the attacker to change directions or to hesitate with the dribble.

Option ▶ Give both players a basketball.
(all skill levels)

Related Drills: 1, 6, 9-12, 21-27, 31, 32, 47, 50, 51, 54, 65, 83-96, 99-109

3 Dribbling off the Wall

Individual • 1 minute

Skill Focus ▶ Ballhandling; agility; hand quickness; ball control; balance; conditioning

Beginner

1. Each player needs a basketball.
2. Players stand facing a wall and dribble the ball off the wall with the right hand.
3. Begin with dribbling around head high (elbow at 90 degrees); extend to dribbling with elbow flexed at 135 degrees; then go to full extension of the elbow.
4. Repeat steps 2 and 3 using the left hand.

Intermediate

1. Dribbling off the wall as in the beginner drill, use only the index finger of the right hand to dribble the basketball.
2. Then use only the middle finger, then only the ring finger, then only the little finger.
3. Repeat steps 1 and 2 using the left hand.

Advanced

1. Repeat steps 2, 3, and 4 of the beginner phase, but while running the length of the wall.
2. Repeat steps 1, 2, and 3 of the intermediate phase, but while running the length of the wall.

Teaching Points ▶

1. Dribble using only the upper finger pads of the hands (see figure). The pads may be used to dribble, shoot, or pass the basketball; *do not* use the palms to dribble, shoot, or pass.
2. When dribbling, the wrist should follow an up-and-down motion, as if waving good-bye. Coaches, check to see whether a wrinkle is created behind the wrist and then released with each stroke of the ball.
3. Once you start dribbling the ball off the wall, keep the ball at that level throughout that phase of the drill.
4. Don't look at the ball. Look straight ahead.

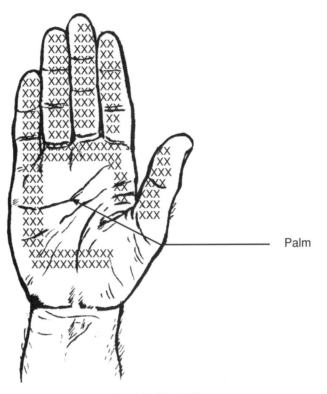

Palm

The hand pads. The ball can rest on parts of the hand marked with X only.

Related Drills: 14-27, 30, 31, 36, 37, 63, 66, 76, 83-95

4 Lane Slide

Individual or team • 1 minute per group

Skill Focus ▶ Agility; quickness; conditioning; balance; defensive stances (97-99); slide step (40, 99); change of direction; change of pace; defensive footwork (97-99)

Beginner

1. Line players up a foul lane as shown in the diagram. Use only three players at a time. Each player is about three feet behind the player in front of him, and all should be facing out of bounds. You can start the players in the middle or on one of the lane lines.
2. Players slide from side to side, using the defensive slide step, touching the foul lane line with the outside foot before sliding back in the other direction.
3. Count the number of touches per 30 seconds. (Each group initially goes 30 seconds. Later in the season you can extend the time up to one minute.) Each player should get more touches each day this drill is done. The objective is to get quicker slides, and thus, more touches.

Intermediate

1. As the group slides, each player executes an in-and-out defensive fake with each step taken.

Advanced

1. Change the sliding distance: allow the players to slide only two steps in either direction from the middle.
2. Change the sliding distance: allow the players to slide only one step in either direction from the middle.

Option ▶
(all skill levels)
Have two players face each other. The first player slides in either direction (player's choice), while the second mirrors the first player's movements.

Teaching Points ▶

1. Players must execute the slide step perfectly. They must not cross their legs.
2. Players should begin with a long step in the direction of the first movement; they then bring the trail foot up to the first foot, almost touching but never crossing.
3. Players need to stay low for better body balance. Lower legs should be perpendicular to the floor, with upper legs forming a 135-degree angle with the lower legs. The torso is straight, perpendicular to the floor. Hands are both out with palms pointing upward. The players must not allow their arms to drop.
4. Toes should be grabbing at the floor, and feet should rise only minimally from the floor. This encourages foot quickness.

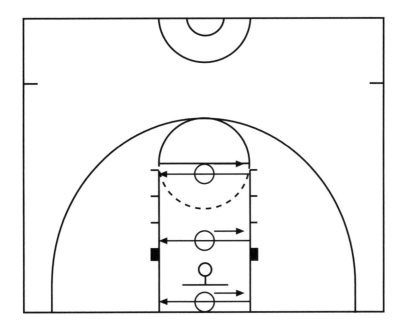

2

Stance and Footwork

Knowledge is the greatest aid in any sport. Practicing movements incorrectly limits improvement and diminishes the level of performance, while practicing correctly accelerates growth, pushing up the ceiling of the athlete's ultimate potential.

Proper stance and footwork are the first major building blocks to becoming a great one-on-one player, to becoming the best basketball player you can be. Without these two skills, development of more advanced skills will be slower and more difficult, and the level of your final performance will suffer.

Drill 5 will teach you the first stance and footwork you need: that for laying the ball in the basket properly, from both the left and right sides of the court.

If you want to be a Michael Jordan and create fantastic one-on-one movement, you must begin with the triple-threat position. Drill 6 shows you how.

If you want to be a Tim Duncan, you have to know the proper methods of getting position in the post area. Drill 7 fully covers that.

You can't stop at just getting proper position. You must know how to make your movement defeat your defender. You even want to be able to coax your defender into making mistakes. When your defender does make a wrong movement, proper footwork will allow you to explosively blast by for the score.

This footwork is divided in two phases: before you put the ball on the floor, and after you start your dribble. Drill 8 shows the rocker step for use before you dribble. Drill 9 is your first dribbling maneuver, the in-and-out move. Drill 10 adds the crossover, a countermove to the in-and-out move. Both are executed facing your opponent. Drill 11 attaches the spin move to your growing repertoire. And then drill 12 inserts a countermove to the spin, the half spin. Both of these are performed by turning your back on your defender. Drill 13 puts them all together, allowing you to create any combination you wish.

5 Basic Layup

Team • 3 minutes

Skill Focus ▶ Basic layup shot; balance; conditioning; catching the ball (38); bounce pass (38); chest pass (38)

Beginner

1. Line players up as shown in figure 1. Begin with shots from the right side of the basket. After 1 minute and 30 seconds, change to shooting from the left side.
2. Begin with a bounce pass to the receiver.
3. Player 2 passes to 1, who shoots the layup. Then 2 goes to end of line 1, and 1 goes to end of line 2. Player 4 rebounds the ball. As 4 rebounds the shot (missed or made), 3 begins to run toward the basket. Then 4 passes to 3, who shoots. Both 3 and 4 go to ends of opposite lines. Repeat sequence as many times as necessary.

Intermediate

1. Repeat beginner steps, but the coach should stand beside the shooter and push the shooter gently as he goes to shoot.

Advanced

1. Do the intermediate drill, but allow the passers to throw a chest pass instead of a bounce pass.

Options ▶
(all skill levels)

1. *Three-Line Layup Drill (figure 2):* Player 1 passes to 2, who passes to 3 at the free throw line. Player 1 cuts behind 2, and 3 passes to 1 for the layup. Then 2 cuts behind 3 and races to get the rebound. Next, 1 goes behind 3's line and 2 goes behind 1's line, while 3 goes behind 2's line.
2. Run the layup drills by not letting the ball touch the floor. This keeps the players hustling to their positions.
3. Let the receiver catch the pass, then toss the ball from hand to hand before shooting the layup or walking.
4. Let the receiver catch the pass away from the basket, then dribble drive to the basket.

Teaching Points ▶

1. The layup should be shot from a high jump, not a broad jump. Go straight up with a slight lean forward. Jump off the opposite leg: for example, if right-handed, jump off the left leg. The shooting hand is always on the out-of-bounds side. The hand should be behind the ball with palms pointing upward. As the ball is released, flip the wrist slightly, placing the ball in the small square above the rim. The ball should not go any higher after hitting the square.

2. To execute the bounce pass, hold the ball in both hands with elbows flexed (one hand on each side of the ball). Step forward as you deliver the pass. As you pass the ball, flip your wrist so your thumbs finish pointing down. Your palms begin pointed inward and end pointed outward. Your elbows should become fully extended. Try to land the ball on the floor so that its bounce will come to the receiver near or slightly above his beltline. The receiver should watch the ball into his hand, then go up immediately for the shot. The passer should be in a sitting position when releasing the ball. (From this low torso position, the passer is ready to make a quick cut.)

3. The chest pass should be delivered as the bounce pass was. The hands should be outside the ball (on both sides) with the thumbs pointing upward and palms inward. The passer steps forward as he passes and snaps the wrists, ending up with thumbs pointing downward and palms pointing outward. The pass should be delivered near the chest of the receiver, who should watch the ball all the way into his hands.

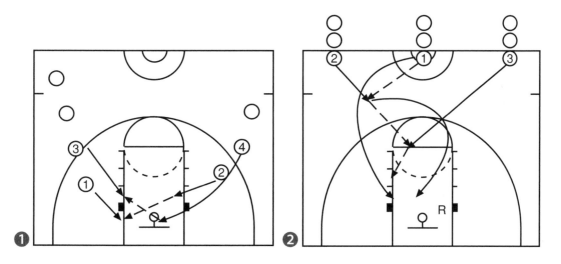

Related Drills: 37-62

6 Triple-Threat Position

Individual or team • 2 minutes

Skill Focus ▶ Perimeter positioning with the ball; pivoting (31-32); peripheral vision; offensive moves (8-12); balance; agility; quickness; foot movement (8); V-cut (47)

Beginner

1. Line up as shown in the diagram.
2. The player V-cuts and the coach passes him the ball.
3. He then reverse pivots and puts the ball in triple-threat position.
4. The player passes the ball back to the coach and goes to the end of the line.

Intermediate

1. After the player pivots into triple-threat position, he does a jab-step fake, a crossover fake, or a rocker step fake (coach's choice).

Advanced

1. After the player does one of the fakes (intermediate), he begins his dribble drive to the basket for a layup, or stops short with a jump stop and takes a jump shot.
2. Instead of driving all the way to the basket, the player stops with a jump stop and does a fake at the end of the dribble (for example, a spin move, half-spin move, or up-and-under move) to get his jump shot off.
3. Instead of driving all the way to the basket, the player does a dribbling move (such as an in-and-out move, spin move, or half-spin move) after two dribbles before driving for the layup.

Option ▶
(all skill levels)
To practice on his own, the player can pass the ball a few feet away with backspin. He then goes to catch the ball, reverse pivots, and completes the drill as described.

Teaching Points ▶

To get into triple-threat position, crouch with a slight bend at the knees and the trunk. Bring the ball up to a position underneath the chin, with one hand on each side of the ball. The ball can be slightly to the side of the torso opposite the pivot foot. From this position, you can pass the ball, begin a dribble, or shoot the ball. (Hence the name *triple threat.*)

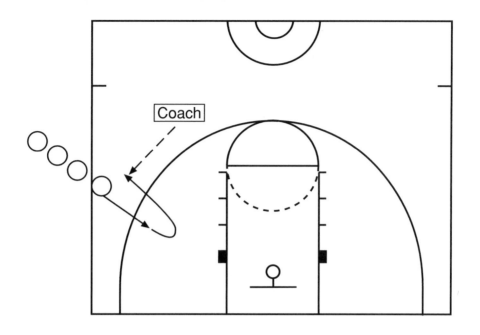

7 Post Position

Individual or team • 5 minutes

Skill Focus ▶ Post moves (75-82); post position; drop step (75-82); reverse pivot (32); layup

Beginner

1. Line up as shown in the diagram.
2. A player cuts across the lane, and the coach tells the player where his (imaginary) defender is.
3. The player reacts by getting position on the would-be defender.
4. The coach passes the ball to the player, who does a drop step for a layup.
5. The player goes to the end of the line after rebounding the layup and passing to the coach.

Intermediate

1. Instead of doing the drop step for a layup, the coach tells the player which post move to use (spin move, half-spin move, face-up moves).
2. Instead of shooting a layup, the player shoots the power layup or the baby hook (based on which move is chosen and which side of the floor the player is on).

Advanced

1. Add a passive defender; now the player must read the defender and set up in the proper position. The player must also decide which move to use to take advantage of that position.

Option ▶
(all skill levels)
While the player is in post position, the coach can race a few steps up or down the sideline, calling out a new defensive position, requiring the post player to establish a different post position.

Teaching Points ▶

1. Position yourself at the big block. If the defender is above you, push him a step or so up the lane—by using your body strength, not by pushing with your arms and hands. If the defender is below you, push him one step toward the baseline. If your defender is fronting you, step once toward the coach. This floor position creates a greater passing area.
2. Bend your arm at the elbow to form a 90-degree angle, then place your forearm against the defender's lower torso or waist and hold the position.
3. Use your off arm as a signal to the passer. Again form a 90-degree angle, but with your forearm perpendicular to the floor. Spread your hand as a target for the pass.
4. Turn your body by making sure your foot on the side of the defender is beyond the front foot of the defender, who is in a three-quartering denial position. This allows the quick drop step to the basket for the layup.

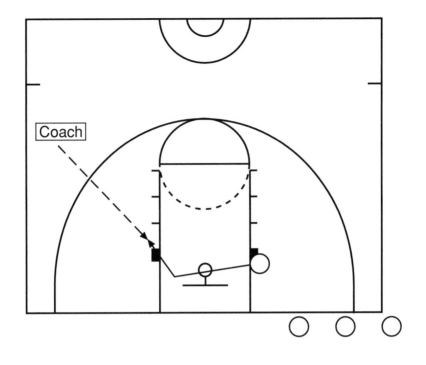

8 Rocker Step

Individual • 5 minutes to teach; 1 minute to review

Skill Focus ▶ Triple-threat position (6); jab step; jab-step pullback; jab-step direct drive; jab-step crossover; rocker step

Beginner

1. The first time through the drill, the teaching part, a player will be at the free throw line with a coach. The coach acts as a defender and explains why a move is made and when to make it, and judges the player's quickness. When the player makes a move, he must give the defender time to react to that move before beginning another stage.
2. The first of the four stages of the rocker step is the jab step (figure 1).
3. After learning how and when to use the jab step, the player learns how and when to execute the jab-step pullback (figure 2).
4. Next, the player learns how and when to do the jab-step direct drive (figure 3).
5. The last stage of the rocker step is the jab-step crossover (figure 4).
6. After teaching the rocker step, the coach lines players up and calls out the portion of the rocker step he wants performed, checking for correct execution. After each call, the coach should again go over when each portion is to be used.

Teaching Points ▶

1. The jab step is the key; drill on it until you're convinced the players have it perfected. This should be a short, hard thrust step—no more than 18 inches, if that. Players should land on the toes of the non-pivot foot, making a screeching sound as they touch the floor. (For this drill, let's say the left foot is the pivot foot, and the right foot is the non-pivot foot.) Explain that a player must check the defense as he uses the jab step. From triple-threat position, the player lowers the ball slightly and leans forward slightly, creating the impression that he intends to drive with the basketball.
2. Stage two is the jab-step pullback. Because the player landed on the toes of his right foot, he is ready to move quickly with it. If the defender gave ground on the probing jab step, the attacker should pull back quickly and release a jump shot. This pullback should not be quite as far as 18 inches. The free right foot must be in front of the left foot for perfect shooting balance. However, the player can use the pullback to get his defender in motion for an ensuing drive, especially if he has hit a few jumpers. The attacker can get his defender rocking with good jab-step pullback mechanics.
3. Stage three: From the pullback or the jab step, the attacker checks the defender's front foot to see how far it is from him. If the defender keeps his front foot near the original probing jab step, or if he races forward with his front foot to stop the jab-step pullback, the attacker picks up his right foot and puts it at least beside the defender's front foot, farther if

possible. The attacker pushes the ball out of his hand to the right of his body. He then brings his left foot forward in an explosive manner, several feet in front of his right foot, and drives directly to the basket; hence the jab-step direct drive.

4. Stage four: If the defender brings his right foot forward to challenge the jab-step pullback or the original jab step, then the attacker should use the jab-step crossover. To execute this successfully, the attacker places his right foot beside the defender's right foot, or farther if possible. From this position, the player releases the ball out of his right hand to the left side of his body before picking up his left foot. He then explodes by his defender in a direct line to the basket.

5. Knowing the *when* as well as the *how* is a must if your protégé is to get easy shots.

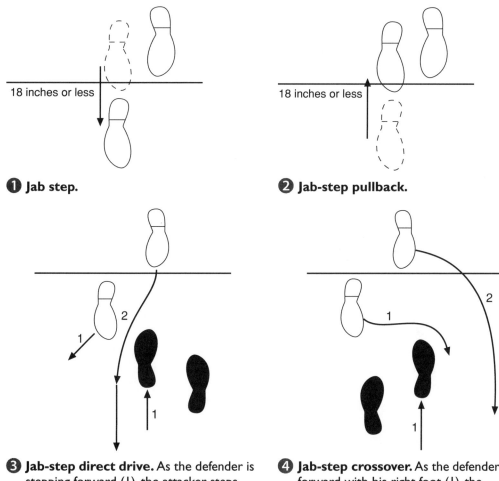

❶ Jab step.

❷ Jab-step pullback.

❸ Jab-step direct drive. As the defender is stepping forward (1), the attacker steps forward with his right foot (1) then brings his left foot forward quickly (2).

❹ Jab-step crossover. As the defender steps forward with his right foot (1), the attacker crosses over with his right foot (1), then brings his left foot forward quickly (2).

Related Drills: 6, 13, 47, 48, 59

9 In-and-Out Move

Individual • 5 minutes to teach; 1 minute to drill

Skill Focus ▶ In-and-out move (24)

1. When teaching, use only one coach and one player. When drilling, line up as in figure 1.
2. Mark a 2-foot by 2-foot square using tape near a line (such as the free throw line).
3. The player starts about 10 feet away and dribbles toward the coach. Start with a control dribble; allow the speed dribble on the next drilling.
4. When the player gets to the square, he performs the in-and-out move. The coach should move in the direction of the step-in fake so he can teach the dribbler the when while he is teaching the how.
5. This move is the complement of the crossover.

Teaching Points ▶

1. Use the in-and-out move when your defender plays you straight up. You may also use the move to get your defender moving away from your intended move, or when your fakes get your defender to put his foot forward on the same side you are dribbling.
2. When you step in, fake in with the head and shoulders, and bring the ball in as you step in. To perform this without losing control of the ball, cup your hand and put it on the side of the ball, knowing you intend to place your hand on the other side of the ball as soon as it bounces back up. For example, if you step in with the left foot, your right hand is the dribbling hand. Cup it from the right side of the ball and swing it through moderately low before taking the same right hand and quickly pulling the ball back to the right. You may actually switch hands while dribbling in if the defender is far enough away so he cannot swipe at the dribble and deflect it.
3. While stepping in and faking with the ball and the head and shoulders, plant your left foot (using the toes) and swing your right foot forward with a long, hard step (see figure 2). Get the right foot at least forward of the defender's left foot. If the fake is good enough, the defender will have stepped to his right, giving a straight lane to drive to the basket.
4. Use this move when the defender plays you straight up (not an over-play).
5. After learning to use your strong hand as your dribbling hand, use your weak hand; for example, if you begin with a right-hand dribble, learn to begin with the left hand.

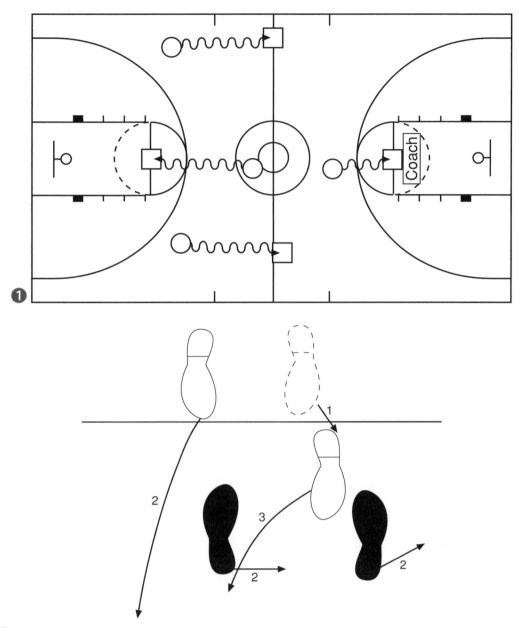

2 The in-and-out move. The attacker steps to his left (1). As the defender reacts by stepping to his right (2), the attacker takes a long step with his right foot (2), then swings his left foot quickly beside the defender's left foot (3).

Related Drill: 24

10 Crossover Move

Individual • 5 minutes to teach; 1 minute to review

Skill Focus ▶ Crossover move (25)

Beginner

1. When teaching, use only one coach and one player. When drilling, line up as in figure 1.
2. Mark a 2-foot by 2-foot square using tape near a line (such as the free throw line).
3. The player starts about 10 feet away and dribbles toward the coach. Start with a control dribble; allow the speed dribble on the next drilling.
4. When the player gets to the square, he performs the crossover move. The coach should move in the direction of the step-out fake so he can teach the dribbler the when while he is teaching the how.
5. This move is the complement of the in-and-out move.

Teaching Points ▶

1. Use this move when the defender is overplaying you or playing you straight up. You may also use it when you can get the defender to put his foot forward, which is opposite the side you are dribbling.
2. Let's say the defender is overplaying your right side (figure 2). Step outside the defender with your right foot, faking with your head and shoulders. You may even dribble the ball slightly outside if you have become an adept dribbler. To make this dribble, keep your right hand almost on top of the ball but slightly to the left top. Push the ball slightly right before bringing it back to your left.
3. As you bring the ball back to your left, lower the ball to a point no higher than the middle of your lower leg and push the ball through with great speed. At this moment the ball is exposed, and the defender can deflect it.
4. When you stepped to your right and dribbled slightly to your right, your right foot should have been forward of the defender's left foot. Then when the ball is brought through to the left, the right foot follows. The right foot should be placed beside the defender's right foot.
5. Your left foot should now be brought forward violently and as far forward as possible while still keeping good balance. Explode in a straight line toward the basket.
6. After learning to use your strong hand as your dribbling hand, use your weak hand; for example, if you begin with a right-hand dribble, learn to begin with the left hand.

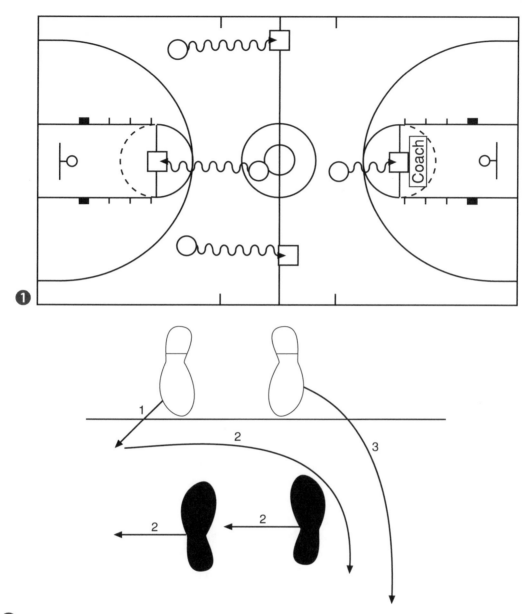

The crossover move. The attacker steps to his right (1). As the defender reacts by stepping to his left (2), the attacker picks up his right foot and crosses over placing it beside the defender's right foot (2). Then the attacker steps forward quickly with his left foot (3).

Related Drill: 25

11 Spin (Reverse) Move

Individual • 5 minutes to teach; 1 minute to review

Skill Focus ▶ Spin (reverse) move (26)

Beginner

1. When teaching, use only one coach and one player. When drilling, line up as in figure 1.
2. Mark a 2-foot by 2-foot square using tape near a line (such as the free throw line).
3. The player starts about 10 feet away and dribbles toward the coach. Start with a control dribble; allow the speed dribble on the next drilling.
4. When the player gets to the square, he performs the spin move. The coach should move in the direction of the step-out fake so he can teach the dribbler the when while he is teaching the how. Or the coach may begin in an overplay position.
5. This move is the counter to the half-spin move.

Teaching Points ▶

1. If dribbling right-handed, fake step to your right. You may also use head and shoulder fakes in that direction. If you're overplayed to your right, you don't need a fake to get the defender moving in that direction (figure 2).
2. Place your left foot equal with the middle of the defender. This can be a jab step with the left foot.
3. Reverse pivot, executing a 360-degree turn, putting your back to the defender, using your left foot as your pivot foot.
4. Cup the ball with your right hand and pull it all the way around as you pivot. Do not change hands until the pivot is complete. Put your right foot at least equal to and preferably beyond the defender's right foot.
5. Swing your right foot all the way around and well in front of the defender. Explode to the basket in a straight-line dribble.
6. After learning to use your strong hand as your dribbling hand, use your weak hand; for example, if you begin with a right-hand dribble, learn to begin with the left hand.

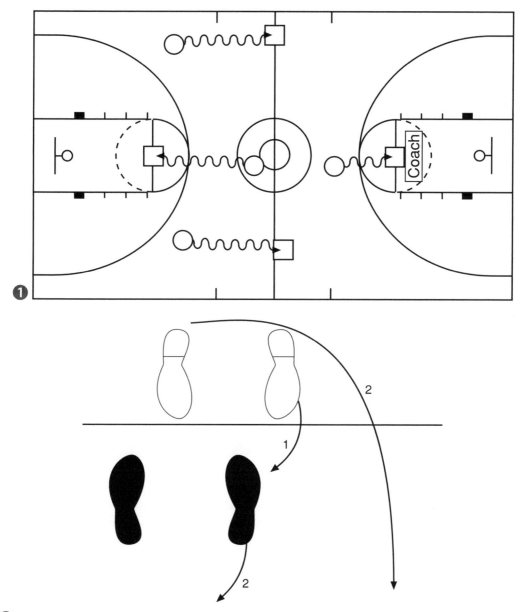

2 **The spin move.** The attacker jab steps his left foot (1). As the defender retreat-steps (2) the attacker does a 360-degree pivot.

Related Drill: 26

12 Half-Spin Move

Individual • 5 minutes to teach; 1 minute to review

Skill Focus ▶ Half-spin move (27)

Beginner

1. When teaching, use only one coach and one player. When drilling, line players up as in figure 1.
2. Mark a 2-foot by 2-foot square using tape near a line (such as the free throw line).
3. The player starts about 10 feet away and dribbles toward the coach. Start with a control dribble; allow the speed dribble on the next drilling.
4. When the player gets to the square, he performs the half-spin move. The coach should move in the direction of the step-out fake so he can teach the dribbler the when while he is teaching the how. Or the coach may begin in an overplay position.
5. This move is the counter to the spin move.

Teaching Points ▶

1. Get the defender to overplay by faking with your right foot to the defender's left foot, also using head and shoulder fakes. Once the defender is in an overplay, place your left foot in the middle of the defender.
2. You want the defender to think you are beginning a spin move, so swing your right foot so your body is sideways to your defender's body.
3. The dribbler begins a spin but only goes about 180 degrees. As the attacker is performing the half spin, the defender is shifting to his right. The attacker immediately explodes back in the direction he started from with his right foot. When the attacker swings his right foot back to his right, he wants to get his right foot outside his defender's left foot.
4. The attacker then brings his left foot around the defender's left foot and explodes in a straight line toward the basket.
5. After learning to use your strong hand as your dribbling hand, use your weak hand; for example, if you begin with a right-hand dribble, learn to begin with the left hand.

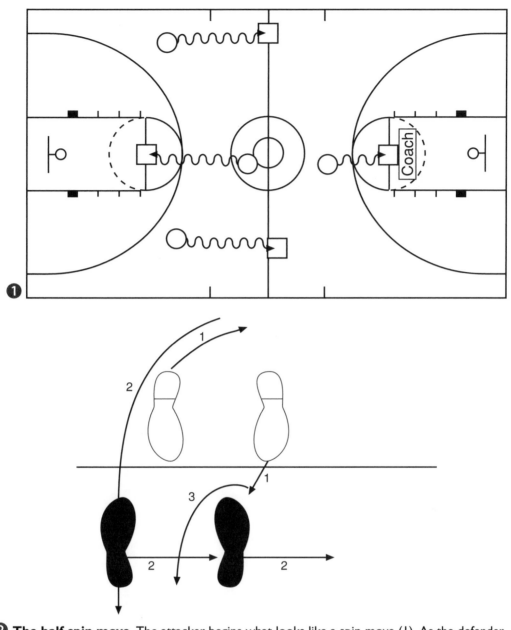

❷ The half-spin move. The attacker begins what looks like a spin move (1). As the defender reacts to his right (2), the attacker quickly brings his right foot back at least to a position parallel to the defender's left foot. Then the attacker brings his left foot to a position beside the defender's left foot (3).

Related Drill: 27

13 Combination Dribbling Moves

Individual • 3 minutes

Skill Focus ▶ Triple-threat (6) rocker step (8); in-and-out move (9, 24); crossover move (10, 25); spin move (11, 26); half-spin move (12, 27); V-cut (47)

Advanced

1. Line up as in the diagram. Using tape, make a 2-foot by 2-foot box on the floor as shown in the figure.
2. A player V-cuts to receive the ball from the coach.
3. The player receives the ball and goes immediately into triple-threat position.
4. The player performs the part of the rocker step the coach designates. The coach explains when that portion of the rocker step would be used.
5. The player then begins to dribble under control to the right, moving to the box, then executes the dribbling move designated by the coach.
6. The diagram shows the drill going baseline on the left side of the court. The next day the coach should move the box to the middle of the court, and the player would drive left and perform the move. The next two days after that, the coach should move the drill to the right side of the court.

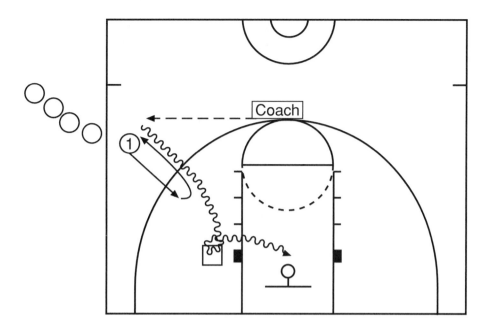

CHAPTER

3

Ballhandling

To become an offensive dynamo, you must be able to handle the basketball. You want to drill, drill, drill until the ball becomes an extension of your hand—both hands. Only then can you perform one-on-one offensive moves with explosive quickness.

The following 16 drills will not only develop that breakneck velocity but also allow you to practice the one-on-one offensive moves so essential for success.

When the ball becomes an extension of your hand, you are full of confidence. You will feel you can complete any pass, drive by any defender, move the ball at will. This poise carries over to other parts of your game. You need this disposition to become explosive in your dribbling fakes. Jason Kidd has this type of attitude and aptitude. To watch Jason dribble and complete passes to teammates in unbelievable situations is a wondrous part of the game within the game. This skill came only after hours upon hours of practice.

Drill 14 indoctrinates you to use the hand and the fingertips. You know the part of the hand that must not be used to handle the ball—and that area must never be used to perform any of the fundamentals of basketball.

Drills 15 and 16 help you begin to envision the basketball as an extension of the hand. The options to those drills will add running, angle movement, and explosiveness to the feel of the ball in the hands. Drill 17 aids in the development of the dribbling mechanics of the in-and-out move. Drill 18 will teach you to dribble and move without looking at the basketball, a much-needed skill in the flowing movement of one-on-one play.

Drill 19 gets the body used to fullcourt, fast-paced action. Drill 20 shows the contrast of playing halfcourt basketball.

Drills 21, 22, and 23 attach dribbling moves to your four basic techniques: the in-and-out move, the crossover tactic, the spin maneuver, and the half-spin strategy. You need a change of pace (drill 21), a hesitation (drill 22), and a retreating dribble (drill 23). These are not only new movements, but also can actually be used when you are doing the basic four.

Drills 24, 25, 26, and 27 are dribbling drills that increase your ability to do the basic four perimeter dribbling moves. Options are offered using two balls, which perfects the basic perimeter move as well as ballhandling.

Drills 19 through 27 all have two-ball dribbling variation drills. The better your protégé gets, the harder he should work with the two-ball dribbling drills.

The last three exercises are fun and competitive drills. While practicing them, you may use one ball or two, and you may work on whichever technique you most need to improve.

14 Fingertip Drill

Individual • 30 seconds

Skill Focus ▷ Develop touch with a basketball

Beginner

1. Pass the basketball from hand to hand in front of your body.
2. Move the basketball from a low position to well over your head as you tip the ball from hand to hand.

Intermediate

1. Dribble the basketball in front of your body using only the fingertips. Use first the index finger, then the middle finger, then the ring finger, then the little finger. Use both the left and the right hand.

Teaching Points ▷

1. Be sure to flip your wrist as you perform the drill. The coach can check the back of your wrist to see if a wrinkle is formed with each flip.
2. Use only the fingertips on each hand.

Related Drills: 3, 15-30, 36, 37, 63, 66, 76, 83-94

15 Standing Figure 8

Individual or team • 2 minutes

Skill Focus ▶ Develop touch with a basketball

Beginner

1. Pass the ball from your right to your left hand and back as you circle the basketball around your right leg.
2. Repeat step 1, circling the basketball around your left leg.
3. If drilling as a team, players should be about 15 feet apart.

Options ▶
1. Line up as shown in the diagram. Give a basketball to each player in the first line.
2. The first line walks down the court and back using the figure 8 movement of the basketball.
3. The first line passes to the second line and goes to the back of the line.
4. The second line does steps 2 and 3.

Intermediate

1. Begin with the ball held in your right hand in front of your right leg.
2. Take the ball between spread legs and pick it up behind the left leg with the left hand.
3. Bring the ball back around the front of the left leg with your left hand and through spread legs to behind the right leg, where it is picked up with the right hand.
4. Bring the ball from behind the right leg to the front of the right leg with the right hand. Continue this pattern of figure 8 movement for 5 to 15 seconds, then reverse the ball movement.

Options ▶
1. The first line races down the floor and back using the figure 8 movement of the basketball.
2. Players do a jump stop 10 feet away from the second line and execute the pass the coach wants to the second line.
3. The second line does steps 1 and 2.
4. The coach may divide players into teams and make a dribbling race out of the drill. Try guards against big men, or first team against second team.

Teaching Points ▶
1. Handle the ball low by bending at the knees and the trunk.
2. Use the pads of the hands, not the palms (see figure on page 9). You can achieve this by spreading the hands until they hurt, then relaxing them. This forms a perfect cup.

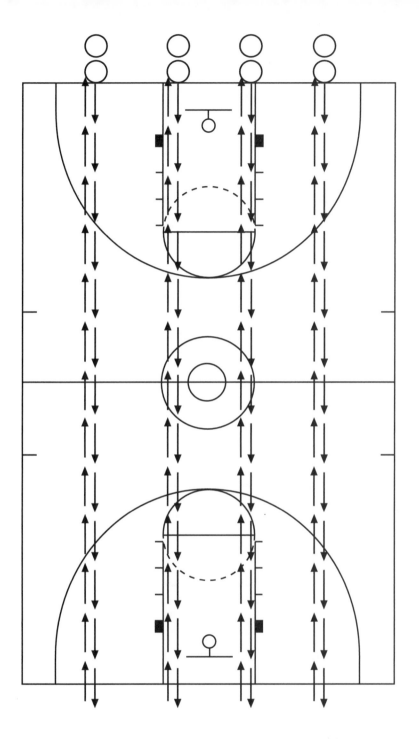

Related Drills: 3, 14-30, 36, 37, 63, 66, 76, 83-87, 90-94

16 Figure 8 Dribble

Individual or team • 2 minutes

Skill Focus ▷ Develop touch with a basketball

Beginner

1. Dribble a basketball very low (no higher than middle of lower legs) around the right leg using only the right hand. Use only fingertips.
2. Repeat, dribbling around the left leg with only the left hand.
3. If drilling as a team, players should be about 15 feet apart.

Intermediate

1. Begin dribbling in front of the right leg with the right hand, then dribble through the legs, picking the ball up with the left hand behind the left leg. Then dribble the ball in front of the left leg and back through the legs to behind the right leg, where the right hand picks up the dribble. From there, dribble in front of the right leg and through the legs to behind the left leg, where the left hand picks it up. Continue in this figure 8 pattern for 5 to 15 seconds, then reverse for another 5 to 15 seconds.

Options ▷
1. Players spread around the halfcourt and begin by dribbling figure 8 in position.
2. Dance while dribbling: move the left foot forward when taking the ball through the legs from the right hand, then move the right foot forward when taking the ball through the legs from the left hand. This dancing motion continues throughout the drill.

Advanced

Options ▷
1. Players race down the floor while dribbling figure 8. This race should begin as a walk until coordination has been achieved. Then players race as fast as they can while maintaining control of the basketball (see diagram).
2. Divide the squad into teams and make a dribbling race out of the drill. Try guards against big men, or first team against second team.

Teaching Points ▷
1. Use only the first pads on the fingers when dribbling.
2. Keep the ball low and dribble rapidly.
3. Do not watch the dribble.

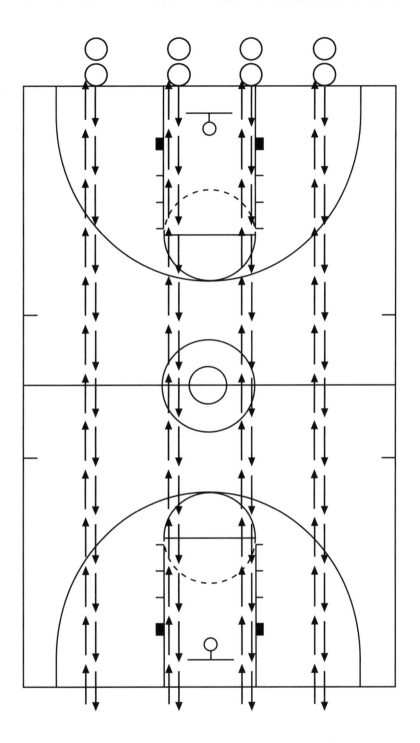

Related Drills: 3, 14-30, 36, 37, 63, 66, 76, 83-94

17 Side-to-Side Dribble

Individual or team • *2 minutes*

Skill Focus ▶ Develop touch with a basketball

Beginner

1. If drilling as a team, players should be about 15 feet apart.
2. Dribble in front of yourself from hand to hand without watching the dribble.
3. Dribble behind yourself from hand to hand without watching the dribble.

Intermediate

1. Line up as in the diagram on page 39.
2. Walk down the floor dribbling the ball from side to side in front of your body.
3. Walk down the floor dribbling the ball from side to side behind your body.

Advanced

Options ▶ 1. Line up as in diagram on page 39. The first line races down the floor in proper dribbling position, dribbling the basketball from side to side. On the first trip down the floor and back, the dribble should be about waist high (speed dribbling position). On the second trip down floor and back, the dribble should be low and quick (control dribbling position).

2. Divide the squad into teams and make a dribbling race out of the drill. Try guards against big men, or first team against second team.

Teaching Points ▶

1. Dribble using only the first pads of the fingers.
2. The ball can be kept low and dribbled rapidly, as in a control dribble, or dribbled high as in a speed dribble.
3. Feet should be spread at least shoulder-width apart. Squat if it allows for a more rapid dribble.
4. Do not watch the dribble.

Related Drills: 3, 14-18, 20-30, 36, 37, 63, 66, 76, 83-94

18 Spider Dribble

Individual or team • 30 seconds

Skill Focus ▶ Develop touch with a basketball; hand-eye coordination; hand quickness

Beginner

1. Line up about 15 feet apart, each player with a basketball.
2. In a semi-crouched position, drop the ball directly below your crouch.
3. Begin with the right hand in front of the right knee, and the left hand behind the left knee.
4. Tap one dribble with the right hand and quickly move the right hand behind the right knee. Meanwhile, bring the left hand in front of the left knee and tap the ball with the left hand. Move the left hand back behind the left knee. The right hand, which was behind the right knee, then taps the ball and begins to quickly move to the front of the right knee. Continue this rapid hand movement for the length of the drill. With each movement of either hand from front to back, the ball is slightly tapped. This tapping should keep the dribble alive.

Option ▶ Instead of dropping the ball and keeping the dribble alive, hold the ball with your right hand in front of your body and the left hand behind your body. The ball should be directly beneath the crouch. Release the ball and move the right hand behind your body and the left hand in front of your body. Catch the ball without allowing it to bounce. You may toss the ball slightly in the air so as to make a better catch. Continue this rapid hand movement throughout the drill.

Teaching Points ▶

1. Dribble using only the first pads on the fingers.
2. Keep the ball low and dribble rapidly.
3. Feet should be spread at least shoulder-width apart. Squat if it allows for a more rapid dribble.
4. Do not watch the dribble.
5. When drilling the option, players should be looking directly ahead.

Related Drills: 3, 14-18, 20-30, 36, 37, 63, 66, 76, 83-94

19 Speed Dribble

Individual or team • 1 minute

Skill Focus ▶ Develop touch with a basketball; learn speed dribbling position (19); conditioning; front pivot (31); reverse pivot (32); jump stop (33); chest pass (38); bounce pass (38)

Beginner

1. Line up as shown in the diagram.
2. Dribble the length of the court as quickly as possible from speed dribbling position.
3. Reverse (or front) pivot at the far end of the court before returning with a speed dribble. Dribble down the floor with the right hand, then back with the left hand.
4. Jump stop about 15 feet from the teammate next in line and pass to him with a chest (or bounce) pass.
5. All players repeat the same sequence.

Options ▶
1. Divide the squad into teams and make a dribbling race out of the drill. Try guards against big men, or first team against second team.
2. Take two trips down the floor and back; dribble with the right hand on the first trip down and back, then with the left hand on the second trip.

Advanced

Options ▶
1. Hold one ball in each hand. One variation is to alternate the dribbles while driving down the floor: bounce the left-hand ball while holding the right-hand ball, then bounce the right-hand ball when the other ball bounces back up to your left hand.
2. The other two-ball variation is to bounce both balls at the same height. Make sure each ball touches the left and right hand at the same time and bounces at the same time.

Teaching Points ▶
1. Proper speed dribbling position requires that you be flexed slightly at the knee and the torso.
2. Ball should be bounced from two to three feet in front of the right knee. The carom of the ball on each dribble should reach waist height.
3. Push the dribble out in front of you, keeping the ball away from your foot and knee, to avoid turnovers.
4. Eyes should be straight ahead and not looking at the basketball.
5. Dribble with the first pads of the fingers.

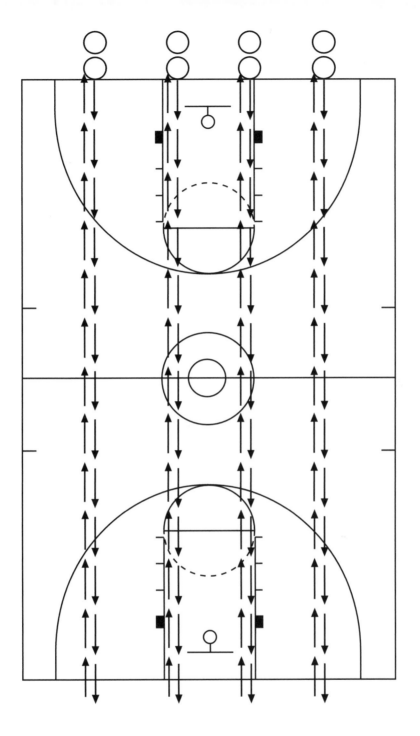

Related Drills: 3, 14-18, 20-30, 36, 37, 63, 66, 76, 83-94

20 Control Dribble

Individual or team • 1 minute

Skill Focus ▶ Develop touch with a basketball; control dribbling position; front pivot (31); reverse pivot (32); jump stop (33); chest pass (38); bounce pass (38); conditioning

Beginner

1. Line up as shown in the diagram.
2. Dribble the length of the court in the control dribbling position. Zigzag a step or so off a straight line down the floor. Dribble down the floor with the right hand, then back with the left hand.
3. Reverse (or front) pivot at the far end of the court before returning with a control dribble, again zigzagging one step off a straight line down the floor.
4. Jump stop about 15 feet from the teammate next in line and pass to him with a chest (or bounce) pass.
5. All players repeat the same sequence.

Options ▶ 1. Divide the squad into teams and make a dribbling race out of the drill. Try guards against big men, or first team against second team.
2. Take two trips down the floor and back; dribble with the right hand on the first trip down and back, then with the left hand on the second trip.

Advanced

Options ▶ 1. Hold one ball in each hand. Alternate the dribbles while driving down the floor: bounce the left-hand ball while holding the right-hand ball, then bounce the right-hand ball when the other ball bounces back up to your left hand.
2. Hold one ball in each hand and bounce both at the same height. Make sure each ball touches the left and right hand at the same time and bounces at the same time.

Teaching Points ▶

1. Proper control dribbling position requires that you be flexed greatly at the knee and the torso. You are not interested in speed, but in quickness and protection of the ball. The off arm should be bent 90 degrees at the elbow and parallel to the floor.
2. The ball should be two to three feet away from but beside the knee. As if you were playing against an opponent, keep your body between the ball and your defender.
3. Keep the ball to your side and under control, away from your foot and knee, to avoid turnovers.
4. Eyes should be straight ahead and not looking at the basketball.
5. Dribble with the first pads of the fingers.

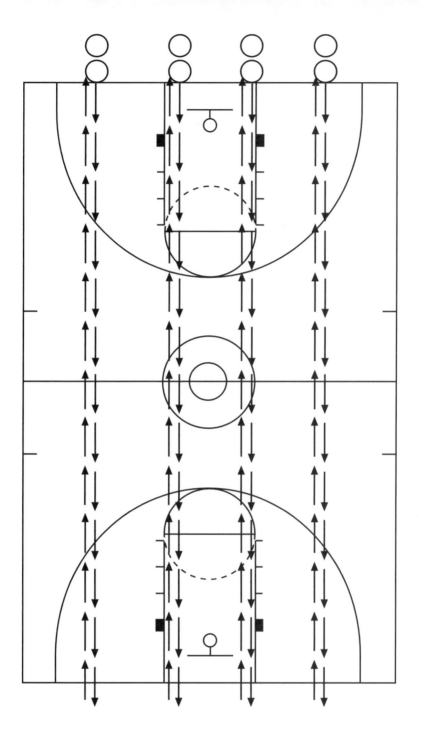

Related Drills: 3, 14-18, 21-30, 36, 37, 63, 66, 76, 83-94

21 ▶ Change of Pace

Individual or team • 1 minute

Skill Focus ▶ Develop touch with a basketball; change-of-pace dribbling move; conditioning; front pivot (31); reverse pivot (32); jump stop (33); chest pass (38); bounce pass (38)

Beginner

1. Line up as shown in the diagram.
2. Walk down the court with a fast dribble, then slow the dribble down; then go fast, then slow down. You can even put in a few medium-speed dribbles to change your pace. Dribble down the floor with the right hand, then back with the left hand.
3. Reverse (or front) pivot at the far end of the court before returning, using a change of pace with every second or third dribble.
4. Jump stop about 15 feet from the teammate next in line and pass to him with a chest (or bounce) pass.
5. All players repeat the same sequence.

Options ▶
1. Divide the squad into teams and make a dribbling race out of the drill. Try guards against big men, or first team against second team.
2. Take two trips down the floor and back; dribble with the right hand on the first trip down and back, then with the left hand on the second trip.

Advanced

Options ▶
1. Hold one ball in each hand. Alternate the dribbles while driving down the floor: bounce the left-hand ball while holding the right-hand ball, then bounce the right-hand ball when the other ball bounces back up to your left hand.
2. Hold one ball in each hand and bounce both at the same height. Make sure each ball touches the left and right hand at the same time and bounces at the same time.

Teaching Points ▶

1. Protection of the ball is a premium, but faking to get away from a defender is also a consideration. Hence, assume the control dribble body position—unless you are trying to clear the backcourt, in which case you should assume the speed dribbling body position.
2. The ball should be two to three feet away from but beside the knee. As if you were playing against an opponent, keep your body between the ball and your defender.

3. Keep the ball to your side and under control, away from your foot and knee, to avoid turnovers.
4. Eyes should be straight ahead and not looking at the basketball.
5. Train your feet to move quickly, stop on a dime, then move moderately quickly, then very quickly, and so on. This is called *change of pace*.
6. Dribble with the first pads of the fingers.

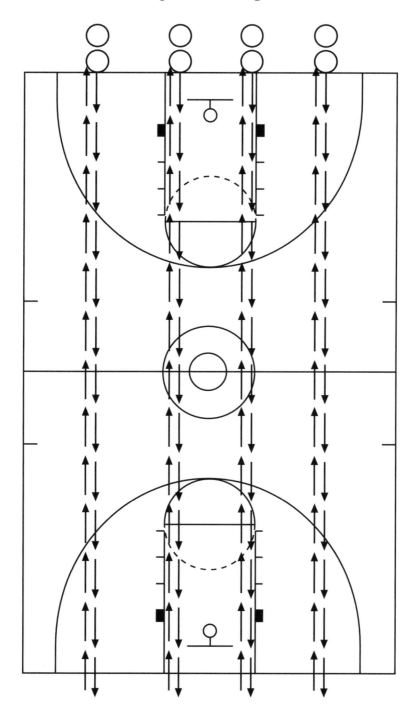

Related Drills: 3, 14-18, 20, 22-30, 36, 37, 63, 66, 76, 83-94

22 Hesitation Dribble

Individual or team • 1 minute

Skill Focus ▶ Develop touch with a basketball; hesitation dribbling move; front pivot (31); reverse pivot (32); jump stop (33); chest pass (38); bounce pass (38); conditioning

Intermediate

1. Line up as shown in the diagram.
2. Dribble slowly down the floor a few dribbles, then stop, and then explode with a quick, hard dribble. This is the hesitation move. After exploding hard, stop, then explode again. Throw your head and shoulders back when you come to a stop before exploding again. This stops your defender before the next explosive dribble.
3. Reverse (or front) pivot at the far end of the court, then return to the other side of the court, using a hesitation move with every third or fourth dribble. Dribble down the floor with the right hand, then back with the left hand.
4. Jump stop about 15 feet from the teammate next in line and pass to him with a chest (or bounce) pass.
5. All players repeat the same sequence.

Options ▶ 1. Divide the squad into teams and make a dribbling race out of the drill. Try guards against big men, or first team against second team.
2. Take two trips down the floor and back; dribble with the right hand on the first trip down and back, then with the left hand on the second trip.

Advanced

Options ▶ 1. Hold one ball in each hand. Alternate the dribbles while driving down the floor: bounce the left-hand ball while holding the right-hand ball, then bounce the right-hand ball when the other ball bounces back up to your left hand.
2. Hold one ball in each hand and bounce both at the same height. Make sure each ball touches the left and right hand at the same time and bounces at the same time.

Teaching Points ▶

1. Protection of the ball is a premium, but faking to get away from a defender is also a consideration. Hence, assume the control dribble body position—unless you are trying to clear the backcourt, in which case you should assume the speed dribbling body position.
2. The ball should be two to three feet away from but beside the knee. As if you were playing against an opponent, keep your body between the ball and your defender.

3. Keep the ball to your side and under control, away from your foot and knee, to avoid turnovers.

4. Eyes should be straight ahead and not looking at the basketball.

5. Train your feet to move quickly, stop on a dime, then explode by your defender.

6. Dribble with the first pads of the fingers.

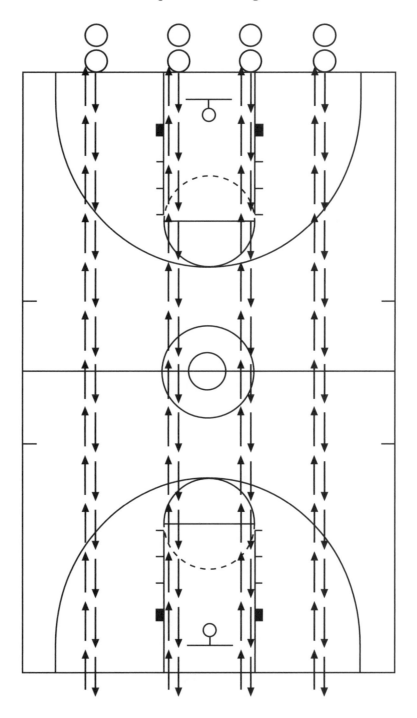

Related Drills: 3, 14-18, 20, 21, 23-30, 36, 37, 63, 66, 76, 83-94

23 Retreating Dribble

Individual or team • 1 minute

Skill Focus ▶ Develop touch with a basketball; retreating dribbling move; front pivot (31); reverse pivot (32); jump stop (33); chest pass (38); bounce pass (38); slide step dribble (76); conditioning

Intermediate

1. Line up as shown in the diagram.
2. Dribble slowly, then stop, then dribble backward a few steps before circling a step or two and going down the floor at another angle. Too often, players pick up the basketball after dribbling into double teams or traps. The retreating dribbling move can prevent this. Instead of picking up the basketball, the player backtracks a few steps and then speeds off in another direction, hoping to leave his trapping defenders behind.
3. Dribble 15 feet or so, retreat, then go up the floor at a 45-degree angle; retreat, then go in the opposite direction at a 45-degree angle, dribbling with the opposite hand, until you reach the far end of the court. Begin dribbling down the floor with the right hand, then back with the left hand.
4. Reverse (or front) pivot at the far end of the court before returning, using a retreating dribble with every third or fourth dribble.
5. Jump stop about 15 feet from the teammate next in line and pass to him with a chest (or bounce) pass.
6. All players repeat the same sequence.

Option ▶ Divide the squad into teams and make a dribbling race out of the drill. Try guards against big men, or first team against second team.

Advanced

Options ▶ 1. Hold one ball in each hand. Alternate the dribbles while driving down the floor: bounce the left-hand ball while holding the right-hand ball, then bounce the right-hand ball when the other ball bounces back up to your left hand.
2. Hold one ball in each hand and bounce both at the same height. Make sure each ball touches the left and right hand at the same time and bounces at the same time.

Teaching Points ▶

1. Protection of the ball is a premium, but use of the retreating dribble must be fully understood by the player or he will constantly be dribbling into trouble.
2. The ball should be two to three feet away from but beside the knee. As if you were playing against an opponent, keep your body between the ball and your defender.
3. Keep the ball to your side and under control, away from your foot and knee, to avoid turnovers.

4. When retreating, use a slide step dribble, keeping your eyes down the floor. After a few retreat slide steps, come out of your control stance into a speed stance and explode away from your defenders. When using the slide step backward, never turn your back on your defenders. Try to time the explosive forward move with the moment your defenders rise up out of their low, trapping stance. You may also use head and shoulder fakes to try to make your defenders think you are going to split them or to go in the opposite direction.

5. Your eyes should be straight ahead and not looking at the basketball.

6. Train your feet to retreat quickly, stop on a dime, then explode by your defender.

7. Dribble with the first pads of the fingers.

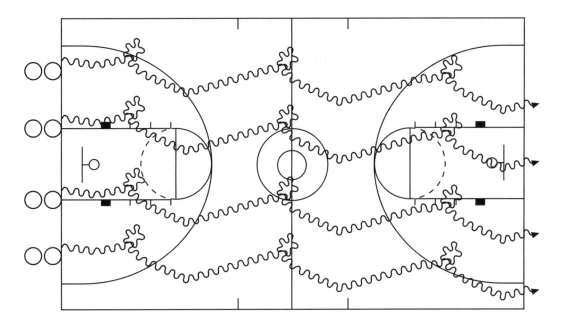

Related Drills: 3, 14-18, 20-22, 24-30, 36, 37, 63, 66, 76, 83-94

24 In-and-Out Dribble Maneuver

Individual or team • 1 minute

Skill Focus ▶ Develop touch with a basketball; in-and-out dribbling move (one of the four basic perimeter dribbling moves—9); conditioning; front pivot (31); reverse pivot (32); jump stop (33); chest pass (38); bounce pass (38); slide step dribble (76)

Intermediate

1. Line up as shown in the diagram.
2. Use tape to mark small boxes (2 feet by 2 feet) as shown on the diagram, at the midcourt line and about 20 feet from each baseline.
3. Dribble down the court, stopping at the boxes and performing the in-and-out basic dribbling fake.
4. Reverse (or front) pivot at the far end of the court before returning, using the in-and-out dribbling fake at each box.
5. Jump stop about 10 feet from the teammate next in line and pass to him with a chest (or bounce) pass.
6. All players repeat the same sequence.
7. Dribble down the floor using the right hand, and dribble back with the right hand. This helps you learn the move going into the center of the court as well as out to the sideline. Go down and back right-handed, then down and back left-handed, before passing the ball to your teammate.

Option ▶ Divide the squad into teams and make a dribbling race out of the drill. Try guards against big men, or first team against second team.

Advanced

Options ▶ 1. Hold one ball in each hand. Alternate the dribbles while driving down the floor: bounce the left-hand ball while holding the right-hand ball, then bounce the right-hand ball when the other ball bounces back up to your left hand.
2. Hold one ball in each hand and bounce both at the same height. Make sure each ball touches the left and right hand at the same time and bounces at the same time.

Teaching Points ▶

1. Protection of the ball is a premium, but use of the in-and-out move must be fully understood by the player.
2. The ball should be two to three feet away from but beside the knee. Keep your body between the ball and your defender. Use the slide step dribble; or partially face your defender, using excessive head and shoulder fakes. No matter what, you must get your defender on his heels.

3. Keep the ball to your side and under control, away from your foot and knee, to avoid turnovers. Instead of keeping the ball on your side, you may fake a crossover dribble, but use only one hand. To do this, bring the dribble in front of yourself with your hand on top of the ball. Dribble with a semi-high bounce. When the ball is in front of you, pull it back to its original spot by cupping the side of the ball.

4. When performing the in-and-out dribbling move, keep your eyes on the downcourt area. Do not look at the ball or the move. Once you step in (using head and shoulder fakes as well), you want to explode when you step out. This step-out should be in an almost straight line down the floor. This should allow you to leave your defender behind. Continue down the floor with a hard speed dribble for a step or two. This simulates your blowing by your defender. Before going into your second box, go back to a control dribbling stance.

5. Train your feet to move quickly, stop on a dime, then explode by your defender.

6. Dribble with the first pads of the fingers.

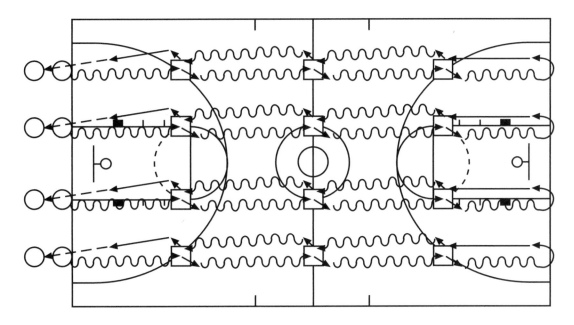

Related Drills: 3, 9, 14-18, 20-23, 25-30, 36, 37, 63, 66, 76, 83-94

25 Crossover Dribble Maneuver

Individual or team • 1 minute

Skill Focus ▶ Develop touch with a basketball; crossover dribbling move (one of the four basic perimeter dribbling moves—10); conditioning; front pivot (31); reverse pivot (32); jump stop (33); chest pass (38); bounce pass (38); slide step dribble (76)

Intermediate

1. Line up as shown in the diagram.
2. Use tape to mark small boxes (2 feet by 2 feet) as shown on the diagram, at the midcourt line and about 20 feet from each baseline.
3. Dribble down the court, stopping at the boxes and performing the crossover basic fake.
4. Reverse (or front) pivot at the far end of the court before returning, using the crossover basic dribbling move at each box.
5. Jump stop about 10 feet from the teammate next in line and pass to him with a chest (or bounce) pass.
6. All players repeat the same sequence.
7. Dribble down the floor using the right hand, and dribble back with the right hand. This helps you learn the move going into the center of the court as well as out to the sideline. Go down and back right-handed, then down and back left-handed, before passing the ball to your teammate.

Option ▶ Divide the squad into teams and make a dribbling race out of the drill. Try guards against big men, or first team against second team.

Advanced

Options ▶ 1. Hold one ball in each hand. Alternate the dribbles while driving down the floor: bounce the left-hand ball while holding the right-hand ball, then bounce the right-hand ball when the other ball bounces back up to your left hand.
2. Hold one ball in each hand and bounce both at the same height. Make sure each ball touches the left and right hand at the same time and bounces at the same time.

Teaching Points ▶

1. Protection of the ball is a premium, but use of the crossover move must be fully understood by the player.
2. Keep the ball two to three feet away from and in front of your knee, using excessive head and shoulder fakes. Or you may protect the ball with your body, using slide steps. No matter what, you must get your defender on his heels.

3. Dribble from a controlled stance, keeping the ball away from your foot and knee to avoid turnovers. As you cross the ball over in front of you, the ball is in its least protected position. So keep this dribble low (no higher than the middle of the lower legs) and quick. Once the ball has crossed over to the opposite hand (left), bring your right foot forward and beside the defender's right foot. Now go into a speed dribble, straight or even veering into the right, as you explode to the basket.

4. When performing the move, keep your eyes on the downcourt area. Do not look at the ball or the move. Once you do the crossover (using head and shoulder fakes as well), explode when you touch the ball with your left hand. Your right side should be close to the ball, protecting it. This explosion should be in an almost straight line down the floor, allowing you to leave your defender behind. Continue down the floor with a hard speed dribble for a step or two. Before going into your second box, go back to a control dribbling stance.

5. Train your feet to move quickly, stop on a dime, then explode by your defender.

6. Dribble with the first pads of the fingers.

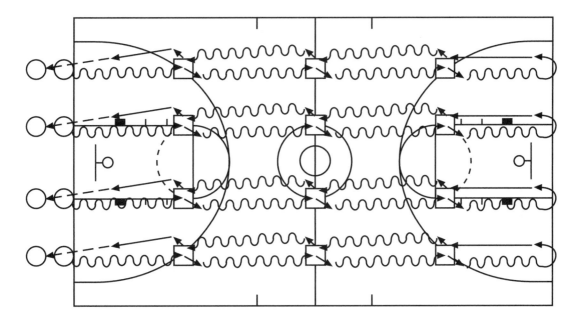

Related Drills: 3, 10, 14-18, 20-24, 26-30, 36, 37, 63, 66, 76, 83-94

26 Spin (Reverse) Dribble Maneuver

Individual or team • 1 minute

Skill Focus ▶ Develop touch with a basketball; spin (reverse) dribbling move (one of the four basic perimeter dribbling moves—11); front pivot (31); reverse pivot (32); jump stop (33); chest pass (38); bounce pass (38); slide step dribble (76); conditioning

Intermediate

1. Line up as shown in the diagram.
2. Use tape to mark small boxes (2 feet by 2 feet) as shown on the diagram, at the midcourt line and about 20 feet from each baseline.
3. Dribble down the court, stopping at the boxes and performing the spin (reverse) fake.
4. Reverse (or front) pivot at the far end of the court before returning, using the spin (reverse) dribbling move at each box.
5. Jump stop about 10 feet from the teammate next in line and pass to him with a chest (or bounce) pass.
6. All players repeat the same sequence.
7. Dribble down the floor using the right hand, and dribble back with the right hand. This helps you learn the move going into the center of the court as well as out to the sideline. Go down and back right-handed, then down and back left-handed, before passing the ball to your teammate.

Option ▶ Divide the squad into teams and make a dribbling race out of the drill. Try guards against big men, or first team against second team.

Advanced

Options ▶ 1. Hold one ball in each hand. Alternate the dribbles while driving down the floor: bounce the left-hand ball while holding the right-hand ball, then bounce the right-hand ball when the other ball bounces back up to your left hand.
2. Hold one ball in each hand and bounce both at the same height. Make sure each ball touches the left and right hand at the same time and bounces at the same time.

Teaching Points ▶

1. Protection of the ball is a premium, but use of the spin (reverse) move must be fully understood by the player.
2. Keep the ball two to three feet away from and in front of your knee, using excessive head and shoulder fakes. Or you may protect the ball with your body, using slide steps. No matter what, you must get your defender on his heels.

3. Dribble from a controlled stance, keeping the ball away from your foot and knee to avoid turnovers. As you spin, control the ball with your right hand until the spin is complete. Then you switch the ball to your left hand. If you switch it too soon, you leave the ball out where a defender can step through and steal it.

4. When performing the move, keep your eyes on the downcourt area. Do not look at the ball or the move. Once you spin (using head and shoulder fakes as well), you want to explode when you touch the ball with your left hand. Your right side should be close to the ball, protecting it. This explosion should be in an almost straight line down the floor, allowing you to leave your defender behind. Continue down the floor with a hard speed dribble for a step or two. Before going into your second box, go back to a control dribbling stance.

5. Train your feet to move quickly, stop on a dime, then explode by your defender.

6. Dribble with the first pads of the fingers.

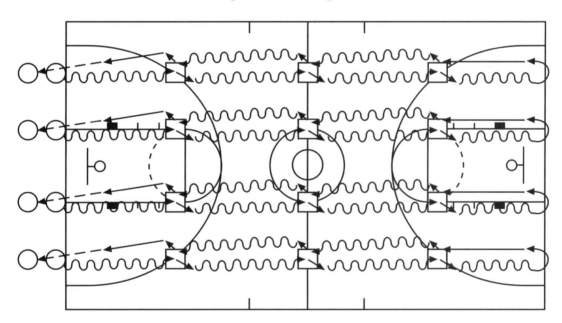

Related Drills: 3, 11, 14-18, 20-25, 27-30, 36, 37, 63, 66, 76, 83-94

27 Half-Spin Dribble Maneuver

Individual or team • 1 minute

Skill Focus ▶ Develop touch with a basketball; half-spin dribbling move (one of the four basic perimeter dribbling moves—12); front pivot (31); reverse pivot (32); jump stop (33); chest pass (38); bounce pass (38); slide step dribble (76); conditioning

Intermediate

1. Line up as shown in the diagram.
2. Use tape to mark small boxes (2 feet by 2 feet) as shown on the diagram, at the midcourt line and about 20 feet from each baseline.
3. Dribble down the court, stopping at the boxes and performing the half-spin fake.
4. Reverse (or front) pivot at the far end of the court before returning, using the half-spin dribbling move at each box.
5. Jump stop about 10 feet from the teammate next in line and pass to him with a chest (or bounce) pass.
6. All players repeat the same sequence.
7. Dribble down the floor using the right hand, and dribble back with the right hand. This helps you learn the move going into the center of the court as well as out to the sideline. Go down and back right-handed, then down and back left-handed, before passing the ball to your teammate.

Option ▶ Divide the squad into teams and make a dribbling race out of the drill. Try guards against big men, or first team against second team.

Advanced

Options ▶
1. Hold one ball in each hand. Alternate the dribbles while driving down the floor: bounce the left-hand ball while holding the right-hand ball, then bounce the right-hand ball when the other ball bounces back up to your left hand.
2. Hold one ball in each hand and bounce both at the same height. Make sure each ball touches the left and right hand at the same time and bounces at the same time.

Teaching Points ▶
1. Protection of the ball is a premium, but use of the half-spin move must be fully understood by the player.
2. Keep the ball two to three feet away from and in front of your knee, using excessive head and shoulder fakes. Or you may protect the ball with your body, using slide steps. No matter what, you must get your defender on his heels.

3. Dribble from a controlled stance, keeping the ball away from your foot and knee to avoid turnovers. As you spin, control the ball with your right hand until the half spin is complete by leaving your right hand cupped over the top of the ball. Just as you plant your right foot and raise your left foot, move your hand beside the ball instead of on top of it. Then push your dribble back in the same direction you came from.

4. When performing the move, keep your eyes on the downcourt area. Do not look at the ball or the move. Once you do the half spin (using head and shoulder fakes as well), explode when you start back in your original direction. Your left side should close to the ball, protecting it. This explosion should be in an almost straight line down the floor, allowing you to leave your defender behind. Continue down the floor with a hard speed dribble for a step or two. Before going into your second box, go back to a control dribbling stance.

5. Train your feet to move quickly, stop on a dime, then explode by your defender.

6. Dribble with the first pads of the fingers.

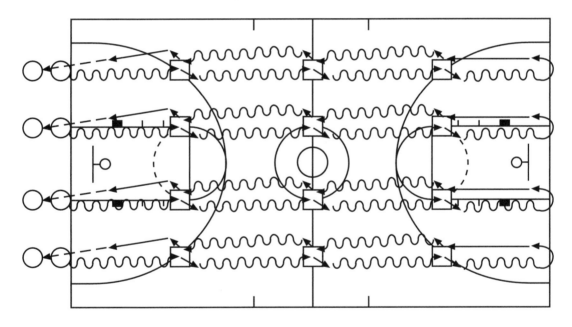

Related Drills: 3, 12, 14-18, 20-26, 28-30, 36, 37, 63, 66, 76, 83-94

28 Fun Cone Dribbling Drill

Individual or team • 2 minutes

Skill Focus ▶ Develop touch with a basketball; in-and-out move (9, 24); crossover move (10, 25); spin (reverse) move (11, 26); half-spin move (12, 27); speed dribble (19); control dribble (20); hesitation dribble (22); retreating dribble (23); conditioning; body balance; agility; change of pace (21)

Beginner

1. Place cones around the court in a haphazard arrangement (see the diagram for one such arrangement).
2. Using one ball, players dribble down the court following the cones.
3. The coach may call out a different move for players to do at each cone, or may have them use the same move throughout the entire cone maze.
4. A second player may begin dribbling when the first player passes the first cone.
5. Instead of using a move to go around a cone, the coach may have players circle the cone before moving to the next cone. This is especially fun when dividing the squad and making a race out of it (see options).

Intermediate

1. Let players use two balls instead of one.

Options ▶
(all skill levels)

1. Divide players into big men against little men, create two equal cone mazes, and have a race.
2. Divide players into first team against second team, create two equal cone mazes, and have a race.

Related Drills: 3, 8-12, 14-27, 29, 30, 36, 37, 63, 66, 76, 83-94

29 Dribble Tag

Individual or team • 1 minute

Skill Focus ▶ Develop touch with a basketball; quick hands; quick feet; aggressive nature; defensive in-and-out fakes

Beginner

1. Line up as in the diagram, with two players in each circle. Other teammates should wait their turns outside the circle.
2. Both players have a basketball. Each tries to slap the other's basketball out of the circle. Any fake may be used, including forsaking your own basketball, to slap away your opponent's basketball.
3. When one of the players wins, two more players go into the circle.

Intermediate

Options ▶ 1. Both players use two basketballs and must keep both alive. Both balls must be slapped out of the circle before a player is declared a winner. If a player has one of the balls slapped away, he continues with the remaining one ball until it too is slapped away.

2. *King of the Circle:* Instead of two more players moving into a circle when a winner appears, the winner stays. One more player moves into the circle to play the winner of the previous round. This continues until all have had a chance to be in the circle. When using this variation, it is best to have the big men on one circle and the guards on another circle.

Teaching Points ▶

1. Keep all eyes up.
2. Dribble with the front joints of the dribbling hand.
3. Use in-and-out defensive fakes to strike at your opponent's ball. Time his dribble—when the ball leaves his hand, dart in and strike at the ball, but quickly pull back to your original position. Imagine that you're striking like a snake.

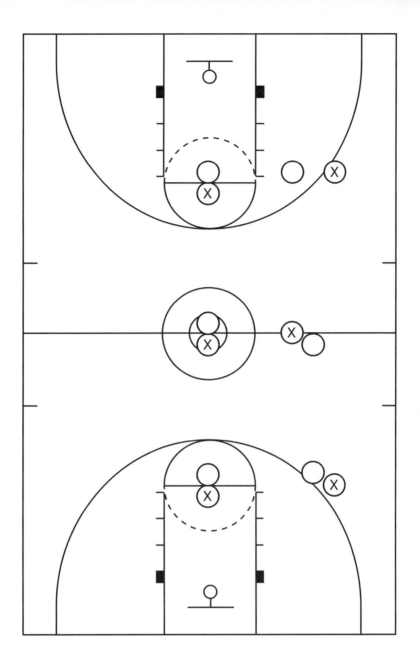

Related Drills: 3, 8-12, 14-28, 30, 36, 37, 63, 66, 76, 83-94, 99

30 Team Dribble Tag

Individual or team • 1 minute

Skill Focus ▷ Develop touch with a basketball; quick footwork while handling a basketball; quick hands; peripheral vision; agility; conditioning; balance

Beginner

1. Line players up with instructions to stay within a predetermined space. In the diagram, that space is bordered by the halfcourt line, sidelines, and baseline.
2. All players begin by dribbling one basketball.
3. Designate one player as "it." He must tag another player, who then becomes "it."

Options ▷
1. "It" dribbles only one basketball, but the other players must dribble two. When "it" tags another player, that player gives the ex-"it" one of his balls and the game continues.
2. "It" dribbles only one basketball but the other players must dribble two. When "it" tags a player, that player is out of the game. He goes to the other end of the court and practices shooting.
3. Divide the squad into two teams. (All players dribble either one basketball or two.) Those on team A try to tag all members of team B. Teammates may double team to get the tag. When all members of team B have been tagged, the game is half over. The coach should time how long it takes to get all members of team B tagged. Now team B tries to tag all members of team A. The team that used the least time in tagging out the opposite team wins.
4. "It" dribbles two basketballs and all other players dribble only one basketball.

Teaching Points ▷

1. Keep eyes up when dribbling.
2. Dribble using only the first joints of the fingers.
3. All players must remain in a control dribbling stance or a speed dribbling stance, but not both.

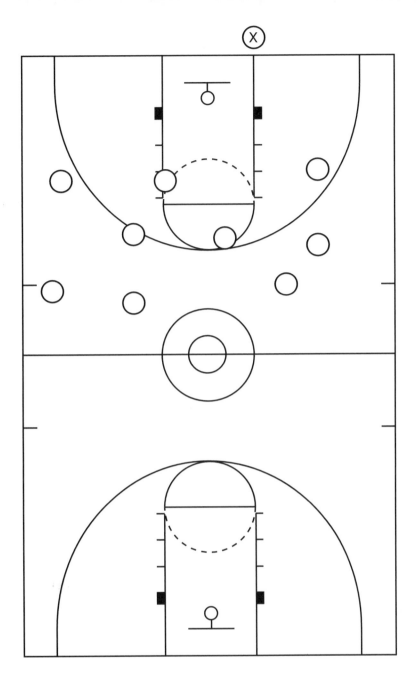

Related Drills: 3, 8-12, 14-29, 36, 37, 63, 66, 76, 83-94

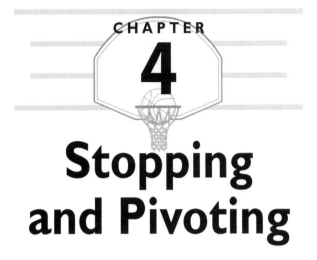

CHAPTER

4

Stopping and Pivoting

Pivoting is one of the most important basic skills a basketball player must possess. You use pivots to get away from defenders; to pass to teammates; and to make a spin move or a half spin. You even have to pivot to screen or to block an opponent off his offensive boards.

Stopping quickly and under control is a must for a great one-on-one player. At the end of a dribble, you will want to shoot—but you can't free yourself for the shot if you don't know how to stop on a dime and go straight up into the air. Or there will be times when you receive a pass that you will want to have two pivot feet. Whether you can do that correctly will determine how effective you are in such situations.

Front and *reverse pivots* are the two types of pivots used in basketball. Front pivoting (drill 31) keeps you closer to the basket; but reverse pivoting (drill 32) allows you to watch your assignment longer and to better protect the ball.

Jump stopping (drill 33) gives you those two pivot feet when you need them. Stride stopping (drill 34) enables you to dribble quickly, stop immediately, and jump shoot all in one motion, making it difficult for any defender to keep you from getting your shot off.

Protection of the basketball from double teaming is covered completely in drill 35. Drill 36 begins the multiple application of fundamentals you have learned, requiring you to dribble, stop, and pivot all in the same possession. Drill 37 carries this multiple strategy one step further, adding passing to dribbling, stopping, and pivoting.

31 Front Pivot

Individual or team • 2 minutes

Skill Focus ▶ Triple-threat position (6); in and out (9, 24); crossover (10, 25); spin (11, 26); half-spin (12, 27); speed dribble (19); control dribble (20); front pivot; jump stop (33); stride stop (34); chest pass (38); bounce pass (38); overhead pass (38); balance; quickness; agility

Beginner

1. Line up as in figure 1.
2. The first player in line dribbles, using a control or speed dribbling stance, to the endline, performing a jump stop (or stride stop) and front pivot before passing to the second player in line. (The pass may be a chest pass, bounce pass, or overhead pass.)
3. All players repeat the sequence.

Intermediate

Option ▶ Each player performs a controlled dribble anywhere on the court. When the coach says "front pivot," each player jump stops and executes the front pivot. On "go," players start dribbling again. Or players may perform dribbling moves, such as the spin dribble, while waiting for the command to front pivot.

Teaching Points ▶

1. Figure 2 illustrates the steps involved in front pivoting.
2. To begin the front pivot, come to a stop, using the left foot as a pivot foot.
3. At the end of the stop, just before you pivot, bring the ball to a position just under your chin, holding the ball with both hands (but remember, just with the pads, not the palms). This is the triple-threat position, described in drill 6.
4. Pick up your right foot and pivot 180 degrees by bringing the right foot between yourself and the defender.
5. The front pivot has several advantages. It lets you stay closer to the basket at the end of a scoring fake. It allows a defensive rebounder to watch his assignment longer (to be used against a quicker opponent, or if you are out on the perimeter trying to block out). It gives you a longer time to view the defensive tactics of your defender.

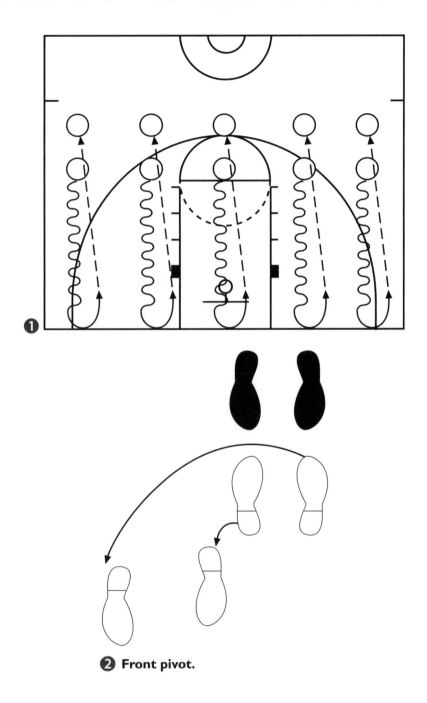

❷ Front pivot.

Related Drills: 1, 6, 7, 19-30, 33-37, 46, 61, 65, 75, 82, 84-95

32 Reverse Pivot

Individual or team • 2 minutes

Skill Focus ▶ Triple-threat position (6); in and out (9, 24); crossover (10, 25); spin (11, 26); half spin (12, 27); speed dribble (19); control dribble (20); reverse pivot; jump stop (33); stride stop (34); chest pass (38); bounce pass (38); overhead pass (38); balance; quickness; agility

Beginner

1. Line up as in figure 1.
2. The first player in line dribbles, using a control or speed dribbling stance, to the endline, performing a jump stop (or stride stop) and reverse pivot before passing to the second player in line. (The pass may be a chest pass, bounce pass, or overhead pass.)
3. All players repeat the sequence.

Intermediate

Option ▶ Each player performs a controlled dribble anywhere on the court. When the coach says "reverse pivot," each player jump stops and executes the reverse pivot. On "go," players start dribbling again. Or players may perform dribbling moves, such as the spin dribble, while waiting for the command to reverse pivot.

Teaching Points ▶

1. Figure 2 illustrates the steps involved in reverse pivoting.
2. To begin the reverse pivot, come to a stop, using the left foot as a pivot foot.
3. At the end of the stop, just before you pivot, bring the ball to a position just under your chin, holding the ball with both hands (but remember, just with the pads, not the palms). This is the triple-threat position, described in drill 6.
4. Pick up your right foot and pivot 180 degrees by swinging the right foot away from the defender.
5. The reverse pivot has several advantages. It lets you move away from the basket at the end of a scoring fake. It allows a defensive rebounder to watch the flight of the ball longer (to be used against a slower opponent, or if you are near the basket trying to block out). It gives you a longer time to view the the cuts and moves of your teammates. It is necessary for the execution of the screen and roll, as a front pivot would allow your defender to get back into proper position and stop the screen and roll. Also, you must get your eyes back on the basketball sooner than you would using a front pivot.
6. Ordinarily, the reverse pivot moves you farther away from your defender.

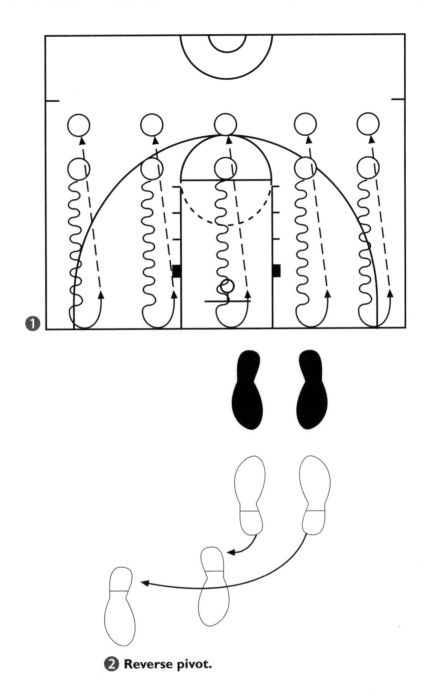

❷ Reverse pivot.

Related Drills: 1, 6, 7, 19-30, 33-37, 46, 61, 65, 75, 82, 84-95

33 Jump Stop

Individual or team • 1 minute

Skill Focus ▸ Agility; balance; conditioning; dribbling moves (in and out, crossover, spin, half spin—9-12, 24-27); front pivot (31); reverse pivot (32); jump stop

Beginner

1. Line up on the baseline (see diagram).
2. Players begin running downcourt at half speed.
3. When the coach says "jump stop," players execute the jump stop.
4. On "go," players sprint again. The coach may give these commands at different locations on the court from day to day.
5. The coach gets in front of players and backpedals until he turns and sprints a step toward the racing team. Because much of basketball relates to a player seeing and reacting, this gives a visual command for the jump stop, instead of a voice command.

Option ▸ If a player is having trouble jump stopping, have him sprint toward you and jump stop. Carefully observe his technique and correct it.

Intermediate

Option ▸ Give each player a ball. Tell the player which dribbling move he is to perform. At the end of the dribbling move, the player jump stops. Lines on the court can serve as points where the player performs the move followed by the jump stop. Then the player dribbles to the next line to perform the move and then the jump stop.

Advanced

Options ▸ 1. As in the intermediate option, players perform a designated dribbling move and then a jump stop. Now, the player also pivots. He then dribbles back to his starting position while executing a dribbling move, jump stop, and a pivot (reverse or front). The player repeats the sequence, each time moving farther down the floor—first he does a move at the free throw line extended, then the halfcourt line, then the far free throw line extended, and then the far endline.

2. Player performs option 1, but alternates his dribbling moves between in and out, crossover, spin, and half spin. He also alternates his pivot between front and reverse pivots.

Teaching Points ▸

1. The greater the speed before the jump stop is attempted, the lower the body's center of gravity must be. To lower the center of gravity, lower your buttocks as though beginning to sit in a chair.

2. Leap off both feet and land on both feet. This leap should not be a high jump, but rather should be as low to the floor as possible. The buttocks may even touch the backs of the legs as the landing is completed.

3. The back should be straight, maybe bent slightly forward. The torso should be bent at the waist. The greater the speed, the more the bend.

4. The knees should be bent from 90 to 180 degrees.

5. When the stop is completed, you may move either foot, for you have established two pivot feet.

6. The jump stop is advantageous because it gives you two pivot feet, so you can pivot in any direction without traveling.

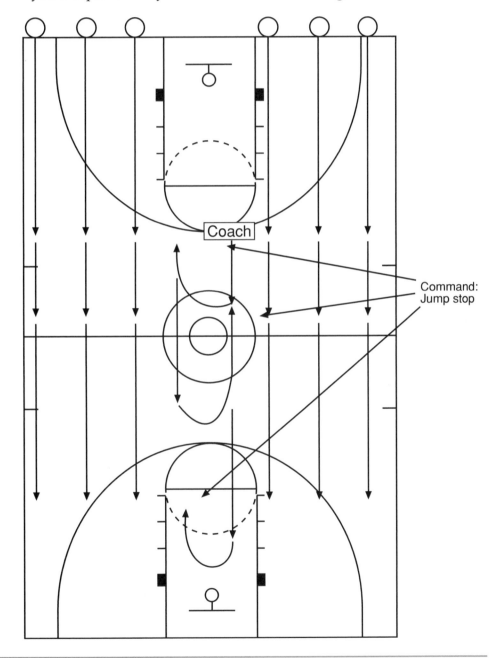

Related Drills: 1, 6, 7, 19-30, 46, 59, 73, 75, 83-94

34 Stride Stop (One-Two)

Individual or team • 1 minute

Skill Focus ▶ Agility; balance; conditioning; dribbling moves (in and out, crossover, spin, half spin—9-12, 24-27); front pivot (31); reverse pivot (32); stride stop

Beginner

1. Line up on the baseline (see diagram).
2. Players begin running downcourt at half speed.
3. When the coach says "stride stop," players execute the stride stop.
4. On "go," players sprint again. The coach may give these commands at different locations on the court from day to day.
5. The coach gets in front of players and backpedals until he turns and sprints a step toward the racing team. Because much of basketball involves a player's ability to see and react, this gives a visual command for the stride stop, instead of a voice command.

Option ▶ If a player is having trouble stride stopping, have him sprint toward you and stride stop. Carefully observe his technique and correct it.

Intermediate

Option ▶ Give each player a ball. Tell the player which dribbling move to perform. At the end of the dribbling move, the player stride stops. Lines on the court serve as points where the player performs the move, followed by the stride stop. Then the player dribbles to the next line to perform the move and the stop.

Advanced

Options ▶ 1. As in the intermediate option, players perform a designated dribbling move and then a stride stop. Now, the player also pivots. He then dribbles back to his starting position while executing a dribbling move, stride stop, and a pivot (reverse or front). The player repeats the sequence, each time moving farther down the floor—first he does a move at the free throw line extended, then the halfcourt line, then the far free throw line extended, and then the far endline.
2. Player performs option 1, but alternates his dribbling moves between in and out, crossover, spin, and half spin. He also alternates his pivot between front and reverse pivots.

Teaching Points ▶

1. The greater the speed before the stride stop is attempted, the lower the body's center of gravity must be. To lower the center of gravity, lower your buttocks as though beginning to sit in a chair. However, if you are stride stopping to prepare for a jump shot, you may begin to slow down slightly before the stride stop. You'll know this spot, but the defender will not.
2. Sprint to the spot where you know you will use the stride stop. Then place your left foot down heel to toe. Swing your right foot forward and

land on your toe. The left foot is your pivot foot. You stopped in a one-two step fashion.

3. The back should be straight, maybe bent slightly forward. The torso should be bent at the waist. The greater the speed, the more the bend.

4. The knees should be bent at least 90 degrees, but never more than 150 degrees. You should now be on your toes on both feet, ready to spring into the air for a jump shot.

5. When the stop is completed, you must not move your left foot.

6. The stride stop gives you a quicker shot. Use it to shoot your jump shot when under great pressure from your defender.

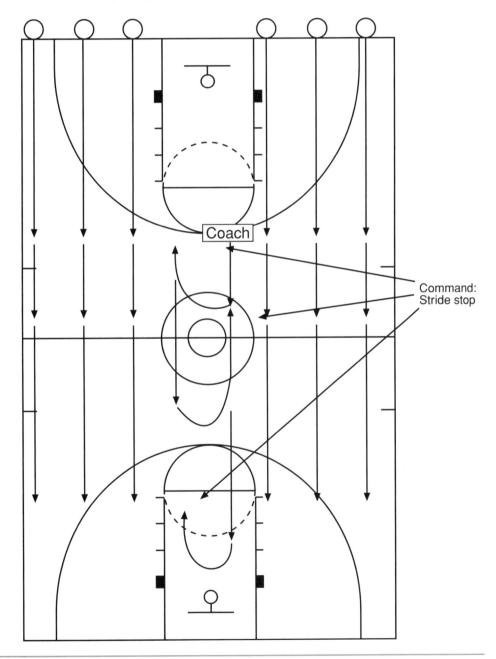

Related Drills: 1, 6, 7, 19-28, 32, 33, 37, 46, 56, 73, 75, 83-94

35 One-on-Two Pivoting

Individual or team • 1 1/2 minutes

Skill Focus ▶ Defensive hand fakes (29); front pivot (31); reverse pivot (32); jump stop (33); stride stop (34); step-through move; double teaming defensively (44); balance

Beginner

1. Line up as shown in the diagram. Divide team into squads of three, each with one ball.
2. The two players on defense are trying to steal the ball. These two defenders may move from side to side in any manner. Their mission is to at least deflect the basketball.
3. The offensive player tries to pivot away from the two defenders, constantly using the low swing-through of the ball to keep the defenders from deflecting the basketball. *Warning:* Players must keep the pivot foot on the floor—don't let them travel! They should make use of pivots to keep their bodies between the defenders and the basketball.
4. After 30 seconds, one of the defenders becomes the offensive player and the offensive player becomes a defender. After 30 seconds more, the defender who has not been on offense becomes the new offensive player.

Intermediate

Option ▶ The offensive player may use the step-through move and dribble the ball twice before reestablishing a pivot foot (or pivot feet) by use of the jump stop or the stride stop.

Teaching Points ▶

1. To execute the step-through move, the attacker needs to fake in one direction and then come back to split the two defenders.
2. Once the attacker has split the two defenders, he swings the ball through, no higher than the middle of the lower leg. The swing should be hard and quick.
3. If you allow the dribble after the split (see option), it should begin with a toss of the ball out a few feet. Now the dribbler runs to catch up with the basketball and begin his dribble. The ball *must* be out of his hands before he picks up the pivot foot; otherwise, it's a walk. The tossing of the basketball prevents the defenders from flicking the ball from behind.

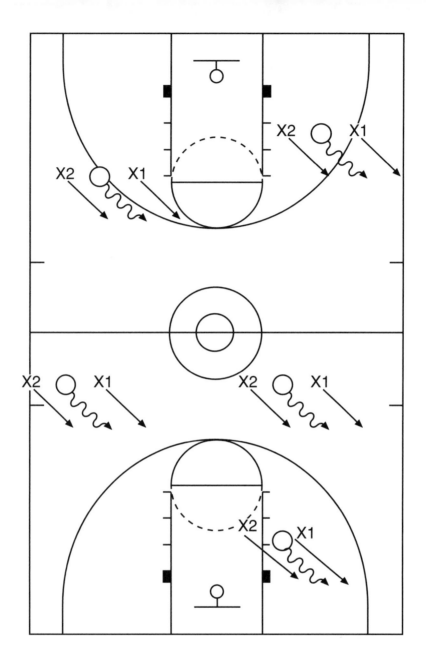

36 Dribble, Stop, Pivot

Individual or team • 1 minute

Skill Focus ▶ Speed dribble (19); control dribble (20); front pivot (31); reverse pivot (32); jump stop (33); stride stop (34); balance; conditioning

Beginner

1. Line up at different spots on the floor, as in the diagram.
2. On the coach's signal, players begin to dribble. They may dribble in any direction, but they should use the speed or the control dribble as demanded by the coach.
3. The players stop (jump stop or stride stop) after three dribbles.
4. After the stop, players pivot (front or reverse, as designated by the coach).
5. The coach checks whether all three techniques are correctly executed.

Intermediate

Option ▶ In a nonstop, one-minute drill, players dribble, stop, and pivot. Then they pause a few seconds. Next, players begin to dribble in the direction they face, then stop, then pivot.

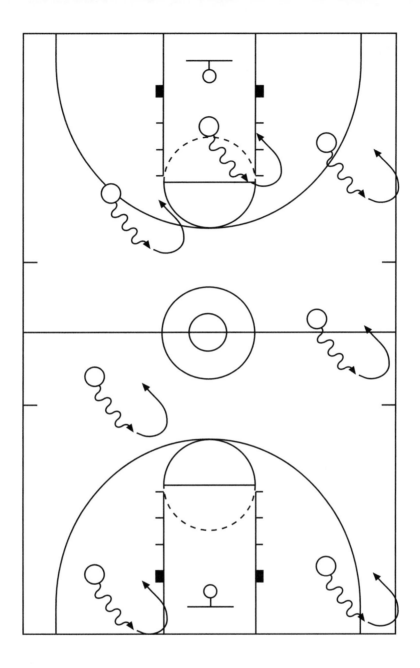

Related Drills: 20, 21, 31-35, 37, 46, 63

37 Dribble, Stop, Pivot, Pass, Cut

Team • 3 minutes

Skill Focus ▶ Triple threat (6); speed dribble (19); control dribble (20); front pivot (31); reverse pivot (32); jump stop (33); stride stop (34); chest pass (38); bounce pass (38); overhead pass (38); V-cut (47); conditioning

Intermediate

1. Line up in pairs of two, spaced all over the court. (For clarity's sake, only one pair is shown in the diagram.)
2. Player 1 dribbles, using the speed or the control dribble (coach's choice). After three to five dribbles, 1 stops (jump stop or stride stop, coach's choice).
3. After player 1 stops, he pivots (front pivot or reverse pivot, coach's choice).
4. After 1 pivots, he passes to 2. The pass may be chest, bounce, or overhead, whichever is appropriate—if 2 is far away from 1, 1 would use the overhead pass. If 2 is near 1, 1 can use the bounce or the chest pass.
5. Meanwhile, 2 has V-cut. Player 2 is yelling to 1, using basketball terminology, so 1 will know where 2 is. Player 2 can V-cut anywhere he wishes.
6. The coach should be closely watching the execution of the dribble, the stop, the pivot, and the pass of 1, as well as 2's V-cut. All corrections should be made immediately.

Advanced

Option ▶ For a continuous drill, require 2 to receive the pass, get in triple-threat position, then begin to dribble in any direction he chooses. Player 2 now dribbles, stops, pivots, and passes while 1 is running a V-cut.

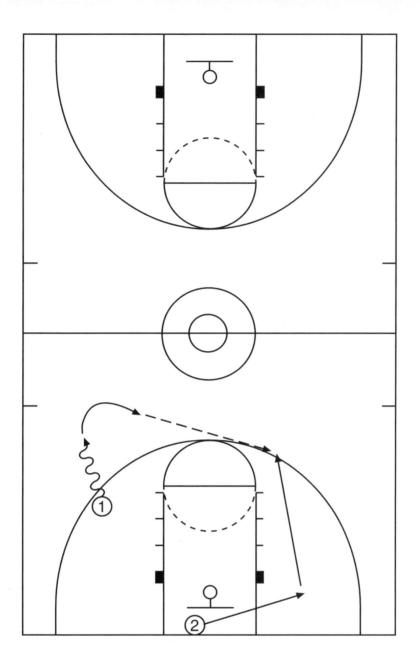

Related Drills: 6, 19, 20, 31-35, 38, 46, 47, 63

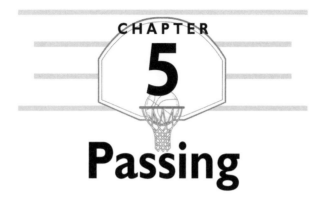

CHAPTER

5

Passing

"The most important fundamental is that of passing the ball," wrote Coach Adolph Rupp in 1948. All he did that year was win the NCAA Championship, and then took his University of Kentucky team as *the* United States Olympic team and won the gold medal.

Passing at times becomes a lost art, but it still is the most important basketball fundamental. Coaches love great passers. They glue the team together. And when great passers are also fantastic one-on-one players, a team develops to championship caliber on the shoulders of one individual. Allen Iverson of the Philadelphia 76ers is a prime example of a great one-on-one player who is so adept at passing that he bonds a team to championship status whatever level he plays. And John Stockton of the Utah Jazz has made a Hall of Fame career out of being superskilled at executing passes, raising the level of play of all who perform with him.

There are three basic passes: the bounce pass, the chest pass, and the overhead pass. Each can be developed by drills. But other complementary rudiments must also be promoted: The art of seeing the whole court at all times. The ability to barely touch the reception before you pass the ball away. The skill to always hit the correct teammate at exactly the right time. These are but a few of the fundamentals that go along with the passing technique.

Drill 38 can be used to cultivate the fundamentals of the pass as well as the art of passing; for example, looking in one direction and passing in another, or faking a pass in one direction before tossing it in another. Drill 39 introduces movement into the pass. Drill 40 carries it to a fullcourt level.

Drill 41 pits a defender against the newly learned techniques and tactics. Drill 42 compels you to barely receive the pass before you pass it. Drill 43 interjects trapping. Now you must use footwork and fake passing to get a pass between two defenders and over or around a third defender.

Drill 44 activates more than one skill around passing. That drill not only has passing, but also dribbling and trapping. Drills 45 and 46 combine all you have learned into drills with movement. Your progress continues step by step.

38 Two-Line Standing Still Drill

Team • 3 minutes

Skill Focus ▶ Chest pass; bounce pass; overhead pass; baseball pass; pass receiving

Beginner

1. Line up as shown in the diagram, about 15 feet apart. Each two-player line has a ball.
2. Players throw chest passes to each other, then bounce passes, then overhead passes.

Intermediate

1. Players throw one-handed chest passes to each other, then one-handed bounce passes.

Advanced

1. Players throw overhead outlet passes to each other, then baseball passes. (Spread the squads of two 30 feet apart for this drill.)

Options ▶
(all skill levels)

1. Players fake a pass before delivering a pass—for example, fake a chest pass, then throw a bounce pass.
2. Players step around an invisible defender to make the pass; step left one time, and step right the next.

Teaching Points ▶

Chest Pass

Cup your hands on both sides of the basketball, using the pads (not palms). Your thumbs point upward and palms face the ball. Hold the ball at chest level. Step forward and pass the ball toward your receiver's chest, flipping both wrists. Your thumbs finish pointing downward and palms face outward. The receiver steps toward the pass to receive it, watching the ball all the way into his hands.

Bounce Pass

Follow instructions for the chest pass, but instead of aiming at the receiver's chest, aim the ball at a point on the floor between yourself and the receiver. From this bounce spot, the ball should hit the receiver between the beltline and the chest.

Overhead Pass

Hold the ball slightly over your head with elbows flexed, forearms perpendicular to the floor, and upper arms parallel to the floor. Hold the ball with both hands cupped, one on each side but slightly behind the ball. Both thumbs are well behind the ball. Don't throw the ball, but rather flip it with a slight wrist action. Bring your arms forward as you deliver the pass. Your thumbs should finish pointing toward the receiver and your palms pointing outward.

One-Handed Chest Pass

Place one hand on the side of the ball and the other behind the ball with a loose grip, using the pads of the hands. With elbows flexed, push the ball with the hand behind the ball. Follow through so that both arms finish fully extended.

One-Handed Bounce Pass

The one-handed bounce pass should be delivered exactly as the one-handed chest pass was. Pick a point on the floor so that the carom will reach the receiver somewhere between the belt and the chest.

Overhead Outlet Pass

The differences between the overhead (flip) pass described earlier and the overhead outlet pass are few. First, hold the ball completely overhead with almost no flex in the elbow. Second, bring the ball back toward your head as you prepare to deliver it. Third, make your pass strong by bringing your arms violently forward as you throw the ball. The distance determines how violently you need to throw. Flip your wrists as you complete your throw.

Baseball Pass

Turn your body sideways to the receiver. Keeping both hands on the ball, pull the ball back beside your ear. If you are throwing with your right hand, keep your left hand below the ball and your right hand behind the ball. The left hand keeps it balanced and the right hand provides the thrust. As you deliver the pass, drop your left hand and throw the ball as you would a baseball. Bring your throwing hand straight forward. Do not put a twist on your throwing hand, because that would deliver a curveball. Follow through by stepping forward with your left foot as you release the ball.

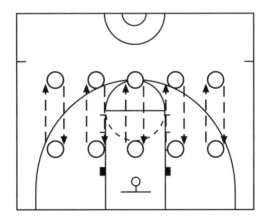

Related Drills: 37, 39-46, 54-60, 62

39 Two-Line Moving Drill

Team • 3 minutes

Skill Focus ▶ Chest pass (38); bounce pass (38); overhead pass (38); overhead outlet pass (38); one-handed chest pass (38); one-handed bounce pass (38); baseball pass (38); pass receiving (38)

Beginner

1. Divide team into two squads. Place one squad above the free throw line and the other squad about 15 feet away at a diagonal (see diagram).
2. The squad at the top begins with a basketball. The first player in line passes to the first player in the other line. The first passer moves to the end of the lower line.
3. The lower line player who received the pass from the upper line player passes to the second player in the upper line. This lower line passer moves to the end of the upper line. This continues as long as the coach wants to use the drill.
4. Have players use the chest pass for about 1 minute, then the bounce pass for about 1 minute, then the overhead (flip) pass for about 1 minute.

Intermediate

1. Execute the beginner drill, but add the one-handed chest pass for one minute and the one-handed bounce pass for one minute.

Advanced

1. Execute the intermediate drill, but add the overhead outlet pass for one minute and the baseball pass for one minute.

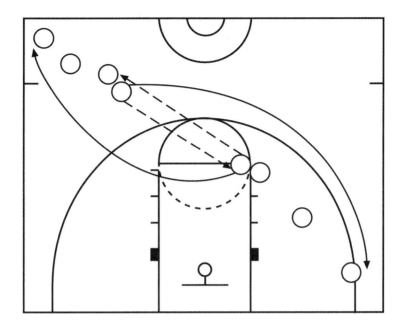

Related Drills: 37, 38, 40-46, 54-60, 62

40 Two-Line Fullcourt Passing Drill

Team • 2 minutes

Skill Focus ▶ Chest pass (38); bounce pass (38); overhead pass (38); overhead outlet pass (38); one-handed chest pass (38); one-handed bounce pass (38); baseball pass (38); pass receiving (38); slide step while running

Intermediate

1. Line up as shown in the diagram.
2. The first player in each line moves down the floor using slide steps. As they move down the floor, the two players from each line pass to each other, using passes designated by the coach. When they get to the other end of the court, they wait until all players are there. Then players repeat the drill, slide stepping and passing back up the floor.
3. The coach designates which pass is to be used each trip up or down the floor. Players receive the pass and immediately pass back to their teammate without traveling.

Teaching Points ▶

1. See drill 38 for techniques of each pass. Make sure all passes are thrown without traveling. Check the slide step for correct technique.
2. To execute the slide step, the player (if going left) takes a long step with his left foot, then brings his right foot up to and almost touches his left foot. Then he again extends his left foot away from his right foot, and this movement continues without the feet ever crossing.

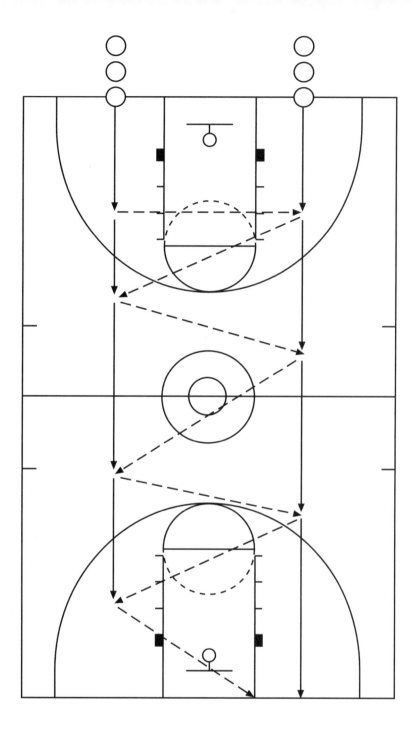

Related Drills: 37, 38, 41-46, 54-60, 62

41 Two-on-One Passing Drill

Team • 1¹/₂ minutes

Skill Focus ▶ Chest pass (38); bounce pass (38); overhead pass (38); overhead outlet pass (38); one-handed chest pass (38); one-handed bounce pass (38); baseball pass (38); pass receiving (38); fake passing; quickness; defensive footwork (97-99)

Intermediate

1. Line up as shown in the diagram.
2. Two offensive players, 1 and 2, try to pass a ball using passing fakes and the pass designated by the coach without allowing X1, the defender, a deflection or an interception. Player 1 passes to 2, then 2 passes back to 1, and so on.
3. After 30 seconds, X1 and 1 trade places. After another 30 seconds, 2 becomes the defender.

Option ▶ When the defender deflects or intercepts a pass, the defender takes the place of the passer and the passer becomes the new defender.

Teaching Points ▶

1. Techniques of the passes are discussed in drill 38.
2. To fake a pass, fully extend your arms as though you are actually making that pass. Then pull the ball back and make the pass in another direction. You may also use eye fakes—simply look in a direction you don't intend to pass, then quickly pass in another direction. When faking a pass, you must use two hands. When using the one-handed bounce or chest pass, keep the guide hand on the ball so you will not lose control of the ball while faking.

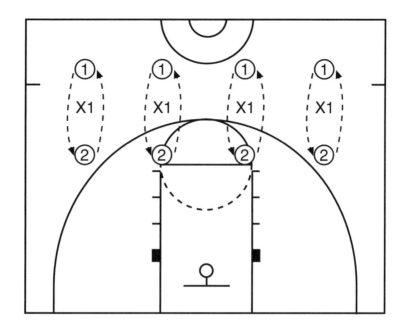

42 Pepper Passing Drill

Team • 2 minutes

Skill Focus ▶ Chest pass (38); bounce pass (38); overhead pass (38); slide step (40); quickness; agility; hand-eye coordination

Beginner

1. Divide players into two groups at opposite ends of the court. The first player in line (player 1) has a ball and faces the other players in his group (see diagram).
2. Player 1 passes to the first player in line, 2. Player 2 passes back to 1 as 1 slides down the line, using slide steps; then 1 passes to 3, and 3 passes back to 1; 1 passes to 4, and 4 passes back to 1; 1 passes to 5, and 5 passes back to 1. Player 1 then begins sliding back in the other direction, passing back to 4 and repeating the sequence.
3. Player 1 goes down the line and back twice before getting back in line beside 5. Players, 3, 4, 5, and 1 take a step to their left. Player 2 steps out front and performs the passes and slides that 1 performed. This continues until all players have been out front.

Advanced

1. Use the bounce pass instead of the chest pass.
2. Add the overhead pass.

Option ▶ Use two balls instead of one. Player 1 begins with a ball and 2 begins with a ball. When 1 passes to 3, 2 passes to 1. When 1 passes the ball to 4, he receives a pass from 3. As 1 passes to 5 the ball he just received from 3, 4 passes 1 the ball. This continues down and back, down and back before 2 steps out front and the drill continues until all players have gone down and back twice.

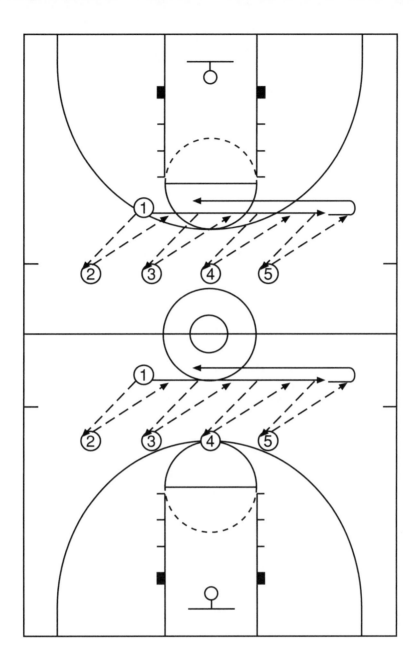

Related Drills: 23, 37, 38, 40, 41, 43-46, 54-60, 62

43 Three-on-Three Trapping and Passing Drill

Team • 3 minutes

Skill Focus ▶ Dribble retreat (23); step-through (35); chest pass (38); bounce pass (38); overhead pass (38); fake passing (41); when to make which pass; traps (44); interception drill (44, 98); trap to follow dribble retreat (44)

Intermediate

1. Line up as shown in the diagram. Divide squad into defenders and attackers. After 1½ minutes, squads switch roles.
2. The player with the ball may pivot in any direction so he can complete passes. He also may fake a pass in any direction before passing in the same or opposite direction. Player 1 is at the free throw line, and 2 and 3 are on their respective big blocks. The two receivers must stay at their positions until they receive the pass.
3. Defenders X1 and X2 trap 1 while X3 tries to intercept passes to either 2 or 3. Players X1 and X3 trap 3 while X2 tries to intercept passes to either 1 or 2. And X2 and X3 trap 2 while X1 tries to intercept passes to either 1 or 3. The diagram shows 1 passing to 3 and X1 and X3 going to trap 3 while X2 slides to a position where he may be able to steal a pass to either 1 or 2.
4. The receiver does not have to hold the ball until traps arrive. Players may pass immediately or wait for the double team. Player 3 may pass to either 1 or 2, and the drill becomes continuous.

Advanced

1. The squads cannot switch roles until the defenders have deflected at least three passes by the attackers.

Options ▶ 1. The player with the ball is allowed to step through the double team to pass.
2. The player with the ball is allowed to retreat dribble two dribbles as a simulation of trying to free himself from the trap. When the player with the ball retreats with his dribble, the two receivers are allowed to move toward the ball three to five feet.

Teaching Points ▶

1. Drill 26 elaborates on the dribble retreat. Drill 41 discusses fake passing. Traps and interceptions receive full technical treatment in drill 44.
2. Attackers should fake pass to get the defenders' arms out of the lane of the intended pass. The coach should check to be sure each pass is made away from the trappers' arms and away from the interceptors' movement.

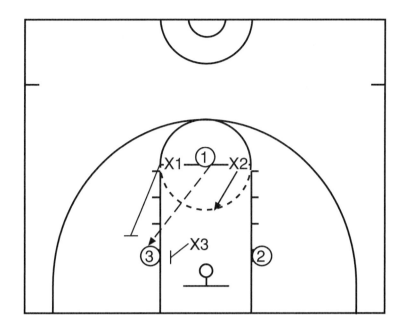

Related Drills: 23, 37, 38, 40-42, 44-46, 54-60, 62

44 Passing, Dribbling, Trapping Drill

Team • 10 minutes

Skill Focus ▶ Step-through (35); chest pass (38); bounce pass (38); overhead pass (38); two players trapping passer; two defenders trapping dribbler; passing out of traps; dribbling out of traps

Advanced

1. Divide squad into two teams: offense and defense (see diagram).
2. Player 1 dribbles into the frontcourt, while X1 stays with him as a defender; 1 seeks to pass to 2. Player X2 plays off 2, encouraging 1 to pass to 2.
3. After 2 receives the pass from 1, X1 and X2 go to trap 2.
4. The coach moves around the court so the defenders will not know where he is. Player 2 tries to pass to the coach, or the coach may have player 1 move about the court to receive the pass from 2.
5. When the trap is over, players X1 and 1 rotate to X2 and 2, respectively, and X2 and 2 go to the end of their lines. Player 3 becomes the new 1, and X3 becomes the new X1. After each attacker has had a chance to play both 1 and 2, and each defender a chance to play X1 and X2, the squads switch roles.
6. You can use the mechanics of this drill—trapping the dribbler as he crosses the halfcourt line and trapping the pass—to build your team man-to-man defense.

Options ▶
1. Instead of X1 helping X2 trap the receiver, X2 races up the court and helps X1 trap 1 to prevent the pass. Player 1 can keep his dribble alive, or may pass to the coach or to 2. In this case, X2 must be in denial position on 2, rather than playing off him.
2. In the original drill, instead of 2 passing to the coach, 2 tries to retreat dribble before passing to the coach or to 1, compelling X1 and X2 to continue their coverage.
3. Instead of the coach calling for the trap to be of passer 2 or dribbler 1, let the defenders call it by the way they play the dribbler. If X2 stays inside to help X1 on the dribbler, 1 will pass to 2; then the defenders go to trap 2. If X2 denies 2 the pass, the defenders will trap the dribbler, 1.

Teaching Points ▶

Trap With Dribble Alive

1. To trap a player with the dribble available (player 2 in diagram), the defender must stay a few steps away from the ballhandler. Player 2 still has the dribble alive. He may split the two trappers by stepping through, but if defenders stay a step or so off the potential dribbler, then the step-through is eliminated.
2. Defenders should be on both sides of 2. Their feet should meet at a 90-degree angle, and they should bend at the knee, but keep their backs straight.

3. Defenders must keep arms and hands swinging in a windmill fashion, with the hands always in the same plane as the ball, regardless of where 2 moves it. This compels 2 to fake again before passing, or else the pass may be deflected.
4. If 2 decides to dribble instead of passing, X1 and X2 stay with him. X1 is responsible for keeping 2 from dribbling by him on 2's left side, while X2 has the same duties if 2 tries to dribble by him on 2's right side. Both have the task of keeping 2 from splitting them and driving down the middle.
5. Should 2 escape either right, left, or down the middle, the two defenders follow 2 from behind and try to deflect the dribble away from 2 (called *flicking*).
6. To trap 1 while he is dribbling, X1 and X2 try to keep 1 between them. X1 refuses to allow 1 to dribble back to his left, and X2 must not let 1 escape around him to the right. Both must keep 1 from splitting the two defenders with a dribble.

Trap With Dribble Used
1. When the offensive player picks up the dribble, both defenders get up against the attacker, even bumping the ballhandler slightly.
2. The defenders' arms and hands become even more active, actually trying to tie up the ball by reaching for it if it is presented. They should continue to keep their feet together at a 90-degree angle.
3. At the end of the dribble, either 1 or 2 can step through. Because the attackers cannot dribble, they may actually pick up the pivot foot to pass the ball. The defenders must be aware of this.
4. Defenders use the slide step while trapping, being careful not to cross the feet.
5. Step-through mechanics are covered in drill 35, all passing techniques in drill 38, and slide steps in drill 40.

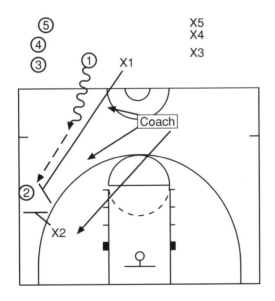

Related Drills: 23, 37, 38, 40-43, 45, 46, 54-60, 62

45 Four-Corner Passing Drill

Team • 3 minutes

Skill Focus ▶ Chest pass (38); bounce pass (38); overhead pass (38); one-handed chest pass (38); one-handed bounce pass (38); pass receiving (38); fake passing (41)

Beginner

1. Line up around the corners of the free throw lane as shown in the diagram.
2. Player 1 passes to 2 and goes to the end of 2's line. Player 2 receives the pass, passes to 3, then goes to the end of 3's line. Player 3 receives 2's pass, passes to 4, then goes to the end of 4's line. Player 4 receives 3's pass, passes to 1, then goes to the end of 1's line.
3. The coach dictates which pass to use.
4. After 1½ minutes of passing to the right, switch directions and let every player pass to the left.

Intermediate

Option ▶ Use two balls instead of one. Let 1 and 3 both start with a basketball.

Advanced

Option ▶ Use one ball and allow fake passes before passing. For example, 1 could fake a pass to 4 or to 3 before passing to 2.

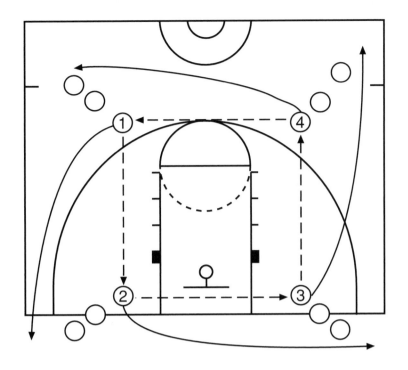

46 Touch Passing and Layup Drill

Team • 3 minutes

Skill Focus ▶ Front pivot (31); reverse pivot (32); jump stop (33); stride stop (34); chest pass (38); bounce pass (38); overhead pass (38); one-handed chest pass (38); one-handed bounce pass (38); pass receiving (38); flash pivot (50)

Intermediate

1. Line up as shown in the diagram. Player 5 rotates to 4, and 4 rotates to the end of 5's line.

2. The manager passes to the coach. Upon seeing this pass, 5 flash pivots to the free throw line, and 4 steps out to the short corner. This gets players used to moving on every pass, a rule of the motion offense. Coach can pass either to 4 or to 5.

3. If the coach passes to 5, 5 front pivots (or reverse pivots) to face 4. Player 4 cuts along the baseline for a pass from 5 and a layup. Player 5 should catch the pass from the coach, front pivot, and pass to 4 all in one motion.

4. If the coach passes to 4, 5 cuts down the free throw lane for a pass from 4 for a layup. Player 4 should catch the pass from the coach and immediately flip the pass to the cutting 5.

5. In either step 4 or 5, the next player in line rebounds the layup and passes out to the manager, who passes to the coach, and the drill continues. This should be a speedy, spirited drill. The coach determines the passes to be used.

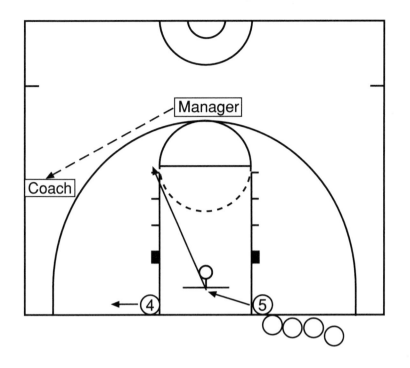

CHAPTER 6

Cutting

You have progressed with your masterful fakes, your wonderful ballhandling, and your superior passing. Opponents will think so highly of you that you will become their number-one target. Some will try to keep you from getting the ball. Others will trap you. Some will assign one player to stay with you, along with a defensive teammate to help cover you when you do get the ball.

To combat the added defensive pressure, you must be able to cut. Drill 47 introduces the V-cut. You use this cut to replace yourself (necessary in the motion offense), to free yourself from pressure, and to keep your defender busy while your teammates score, among other reasons. The options in drill 47 also progress the team offense from just cutting into the beginning of faking, used within the team concept.

There are only two types of individual off-the-ball defensive coverage. Your defender can play more toward the basket, giving you the middle cut (drill 48); or your defender can play more toward the ball, conceding the back-door cut (drill 49). These cuts are also available when your opponent watches the ball or overplays you.

Anytime you are at a wing or lower, you have the opportunity to flash pivot (drill 50). Drill 51 begins to teach the combination of movements—these involve not only cutting, but also one-on-one play.

Drills 52 and 53 get you thinking about the tactics of cutting—the when, not just the how. This is quite important when you begin to operate under motion offense rules.

47 V-Cut

Individual or team • 3 minutes

Skill Focus ▷ Triple-threat position (6); rocker step (8); in and out (9, 24); crossover (10, 25); spin (11, 26); half spin (12, 27); control dribble (20); front pivot (31); stride stop (34); chest pass (38); bounce pass (38); pass receiving (38); slide step (40); fake passing (41); V-cut; swim technique; sealing technique

Beginner

1. Line up as in figure 1.
2. Player 2 V-cuts to get himself open.
3. Player 1 passes to 2, then goes to the end of 2's line.
4. Player 3 V-cuts to get himself open.
5. Player 2 passes to 3, then goes to the end of 3's line.
6. This procedure continues as long as the coach wants.
7. Drill on the right side of the court one day, and on the left side the next.

Option ▷ To teach the V-cut to an individual, set up a cone for the player to cut around. Have the player make the cut, then pass the ball to him. Correct his cutting technique, get the ball back from him, and repeat the process as long as you think is necessary.

Intermediate

Options ▷ 1. Players execute the drill at various places over the halfcourt and the fullcourt.
2. Players complete the V-cut by using a sealing maneuver.

V-Cut Into Triple-Threat Position

1. Line up as shown in figure 2.
2. Player 2 makes a V-cut.
3. Coach passes 2 the ball. Upon receiving the ball, 2 front pivots into triple-threat position.
4. Player 2 executes the offensive fake the coach demands, then goes to the end of the line.
5. Drill on the right side of the court one day and on the left side the next.

Advanced

Options ▷ 1. Add a defender to play only token defense. (Or the coach may serve as the defender.) This allows the players to see how the V-cut should actually work in the course of a game.

V-Cut Into Triple-Threat Position

1. Add a token defensive player. Player 2 must read the defender's stance and actions and make his move according to what the defender has dictated.

2. The coach, without allowing a defender, calls for multiple options on the fakes: for example, the jab-step crossover into a dribbling half spin.

Teaching Points ▶

1. This is the beginning of the development of the team motion offense.
2. The V-cut is used in four options:
   a. To free yourself for a pass, to continue the swing of the ball from one side of the court to the other
   b. To get yourself open at the wing to begin your offense
   c. To keep your defender busy by merely replacing yourself in the scheme of the motion offense while your teammates attack
   d. To try to coax your defender into an individual defensive mistake, such as playing too far off the line of the ball (see back-door cut) or playing too close to you (see middle cut)
3. To V-cut, you want to change your pace. In figure 2, for example, 2 would walk slowly toward the baseline. Once he decides to make his cut, he plants his inside foot (left foot in figure 2) and front pivots with a long step with his right foot in the direction he came from. He now races back outside, giving his left hand and arm as a target for 1 to make his pass. Or, instead of racing back outside, 1 could slide step back outside. Player 1 should lead 2 a step or so. He (1) could use either the chest pass or the bounce pass. Instead of walking in and then cutting hard back outside, 2 could jog in and then break hard outside. Any change of pace will do.
4. To use the sealing technique, 2 stops on his inside foot (the left foot in figure 2),using the stride stop. He then picks up his right foot and front pivots bringing his right foot between his torso and his defender. He also uses the swim move with his right arm, meaning that he swings his right arm between his torso and his defender and then propels his right arm in a swim motion without pushing. He now holds this arm against his defender while he slides back outside to receive the pass.

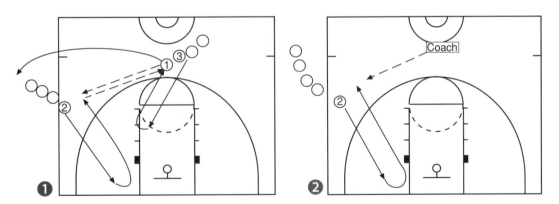

Related Drills: 31, 34, 38, 40, 41, 52-55, 57, 58, 90-95

48 Middle Cut

Individual or team • 3 minutes

Skill Focus ▶ Basic layup (5); in and out (9, 24); crossover (10, 25); spin (11, 26); half spin (12, 27); front pivot (31); stride stop (34); chest pass (38); bounce pass (38); overhead pass (38); pass receiving (38); slide step (40); middle cut; slide dribble (76)

Beginner

1. Line up as shown in figure 1.
2. Player 1 makes a middle cut around a cone.
3. The coach passes the ball to 1, and he slide dribbles to a point outside the lane and passes the ball back to the coach. Player 1 uses the chest, bounce, or overhead pass, whichever the coach wants to work on. (It is usually best to use either the bounce or the overhead, preceded by a fake of the one you do not intend to use.)
4. Player 1 goes to the end of the line, while the next player in line steps up to make the middle cut.
5. Drill on the right side of the court one day and on the left side the next.

Option ▶ To teach the middle cut to an individual, set up a cone for the player to cut around. Have the player make the cut, then pass the ball to him. Correct his cutting technique, get the ball back from him, and repeat the process as long as you think is necessary.

Intermediate

Options ▶
1. Instead of passing to the cutter, the coach fakes a pass and allows the cutter to cut all the way through to the corner.
2. Instead of using a cone, use a token defender. This defender should step in the direction of the fake and follow the attacker to the basket.

Middle Cut and Layup

1. Line up as shown in figure 2.
2. Player 1 passes to 2, then middle cuts.
3. Then 2 passes to 1 for the driving layup. The coach rebounds 1's shot and passes to 2, then 1 goes to the end of 2's line.
4. Player 2 passes to 3, then middle cuts.
5. Player 3 passes to 2 for the driving layup. The coach rebounds 2's shot and passes to 3, then 2 goes to the end of 3's line.
6. This procedure continues for as long as the coach wants to run the drill.
7. Drill on the right side of the court one day and on the left side the next.

Option ▸ *Middle Cut and Layup*

Each player has a basketball and rebounds his own shot. Then the player dribbles back out to the end of his designated line. While dribbling back out to the end of the designated line, the player executes a dribbling move (such as the spin).

Teaching Points ▸

1. The middle cut should be used anytime the cutter sees that his defender is *not* playing in a jump step toward the ball defensive position. That is the beauty of the motion offense: a player may cut when he sees the defender is making a mistake instead of having to wait for the pattern to develop.

2. When making the middle cut, the cutter will usually receive the pass. But should the player not receive the pass, the cutter should continue on through the lane to the corner. This clears out the scoring area for the next cutter.

3. To execute the middle cut, 1 first recognizes that his defender is not between him and the basketball. He then steps one step opposite the direction of his cut. This step should be a stride stop. In figure 1, 1 stops on his right foot. He then takes a long step with his left foot, swinging his right foot in a front pivot between himself and his defender. Player 1's defender should now be on his back. Player 1 should commence using slide steps to keep his defender on his back. Should 1 receive the pass, he uses the slide dribble and steps slightly into his defender as he drives for the layup. The defender is out of position and must foul 1 or concede the layup. If 1 jumps slightly back toward his defender, it usually ends in a three-point play.

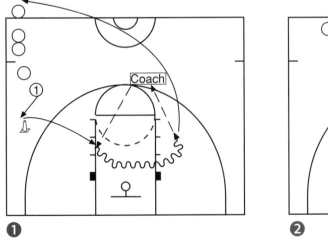

❶

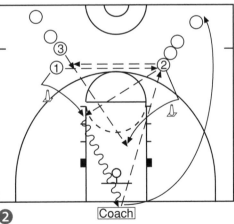

❷

Related Drills: 31, 34, 38, 40, 52-55, 57, 58, 62, 76, 90-95

49 Back-Door Cut

Individual or team • 3 minutes

Skill Focus ▶ Basic layup (5); in and out (9, 24); crossover (10, 25); spin (11, 26); half spin (12, 27); front pivot (31); reverse pivot (32); jump stop (33); stride stop (34); chest pass (38); bounce pass (38); overhead pass (38); pass receiving (38); fake passing (41); swim move (47); V-cut (47); back-door cut; fakes at end of dribble (75)

Beginner

1. Line up as shown in figure 1.
2. Player 2 steps once or twice toward the cone and plants his outside foot (right foot in figure 1), using the stride stop.
3. Player 2 front pivots and crosses over his left foot, using his right foot as his pivot foot, then blasts hard toward the basket.
4. The coach passes to 2, who gives a hand target, for the drive into the corner.
5. Player 2 passes to the coach, then goes to the end of the line.
6. Drill on the right side of the court one day and on the left side the next.

Option ▶ To teach the back-door cut to an individual, set up a cone for the player to cut around. Have the player make the cut, then pass the ball to him. Correct his cutting technique, get the ball back from him, and repeat the process as long as you think is necessary.

Intermediate

Options ▶ *Back-Door Cut and Layup*

1. Line up as shown in figure 2.
2. Player 1 fakes and then back-door cuts around the cone; 2 passes 1 the ball.
3. Player 1 drives for a layup. The coach retrieves the ball and passes to 3, while 1 goes to the end of line 2.
4. Player 2 fakes a step toward his cone, then back-door cuts.
5. Player 3 passes to 2 for a driving layup. The coach retrieves the ball and passes to 4, while 2 goes to the end of line 3.
6. This procedure continues for as long as the coach wants to run the drill.

Advanced

Options ▶ 1. Player 2 drives toward the corner and uses a dribbling move. After driving to the corner, he reverse pivots and passes back to the coach, using a pass designated by the coach.

Back-Door Cut and Layup

1. Instead of shooting a layup, the cutter does a jump stop at the basket area, simulating the presence of a helping defender rotating over to stop the layup. At the end of the jump stop, the cutter uses a move at the end of the dribble (pump fake, pump-fake crossover, pump-fake spin, pump-fake half spin, all explained in drill 75).
2. Instead of shooting the layup or doing the previous option, the cutter dribbles out to the corner, performs a dribbling move, then throws an outlet pass to the same line he came from.

Teaching Points ▶

1. Use the back-door cut any time you are overplayed or the area you're in needs to be cleared out to keep the motion offense going. You may also use it any time your defender has not dropped at least one step off the line between the cutter and the ball.
2. You can get the layup if, during an overplay, the defender's knee comes over his toe. This means the defender is off-balance and cannot recover to stop the back-door cut.
3. If you intend to go back-door, you must give your teammate a signal. The best one to use is the closed fist. Give this signal with the hand on the side where you are being overplayed.
4. To successfully execute the back-door cut, step toward the defender a step or two, then use the stride stop, front pivoting with the back foot as the pivot foot. Then cut hard and in a straight line to the basket. Use your front hand, open with the palm pointing toward the passer, as a target hand.

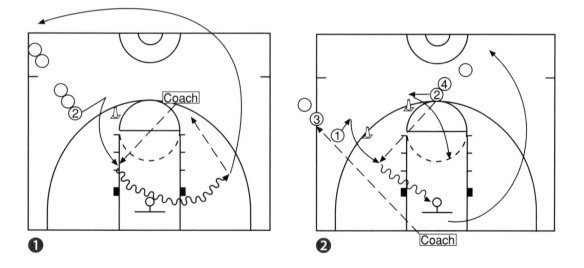

Related Drills: 9-12, 24-27, 31, 32, 34, 38, 40, 48, 52-58, 62, 90-95

50 Flash Pivot Cutting

Individual or team • 3 minutes

Skill Focus ▶ Triple-threat position (6); front pivot (31); reverse pivot (32); chest pass (38); bounce pass (38); overhead pass (38); pass receiving (38); slide step (40); swim move (47); middle cut (48); back-door cut (49); flash pivot cut; drop step (75); fence slide (96)

Beginner

1. Line up as shown in figure 1.
2. Use a token defender to teach the correct spot to begin the flash pivot cut.
3. Player 1 walks in toward the basket until he gets X1 in a direct line between himself and the passer (coach). At this point, 1 pushes off his outside foot (left foot in figure 1) and sprints out of the lane. This is the technique of the cut without a seal. The cutter could end up at the free throw line, top of the key, or any high post-side position.
4. Player 1 receives the pass and passes back to the coach, then goes to the end of the line.

Options ▶ *Flash Pivot and Triple-Threat Position*

1. Line up as shown in figure 2.
2. Player 1 flash pivots and receives a pass from 2.
3. Player 1 immediately front pivots into triple-threat position.
4. Then 1 passes to 4 and goes to the end of line 4, and 2 goes to the end of line 3.
5. Player 3 flash pivots and the drill continues until the coach stops it.

Intermediate

Options ▶ 1. Run the same drill, but allow the defender to overplay the cut to the free throw line using the fence slide maneuver. This compels the receiver to run the middle cut and teaches the receiver to recognize when the middle cut is available. The coach then hits the cutter for a layup.
2. Run the same drill but allow the defender to overplay the cut by getting in the line between the receiver and the passer. This compels the cutter to immediately run the back-door cut and teaches the receiver to recognize when the back-door cut is available. The coach then hits the cutter for a layup.

Flash Pivot and Triple-Threat Position

1. The defender, X1, overplays as 1 receives a pass from 2. X1 simulates a steal. Upon reception, 1 drop steps, using the reverse pivot, and drives for a layup. X1 should be the coach or a manager.
2. X1 mixes up his coverage. One time he overplays; next time he allows the reception and plays straight up. Player 1 must recognize the coverage and react accordingly: drop step if overplayed, or triple threat if allowed to get the ball.

Teaching Points ▶

1. To execute the flash pivot cut, walk your defender to a spot where the defender can no longer see both the passer and the cutter. At that exact moment, change direction and pace by sprinting out to the high-post area. This can be at the top of the key, at the free throw line, or at any high-post position. When you change direction, push off your inside foot, make incidental contact with the defender, front pivot, and use the swim move. This is the cut using a seal. The sprint out to the high post should use the slide step maneuver to keep the defender on the cutter's back.

2. When you reach the area where you intend to receive the pass, you may either stride stop (one pivot foot) or jump stop (two pivot feet).

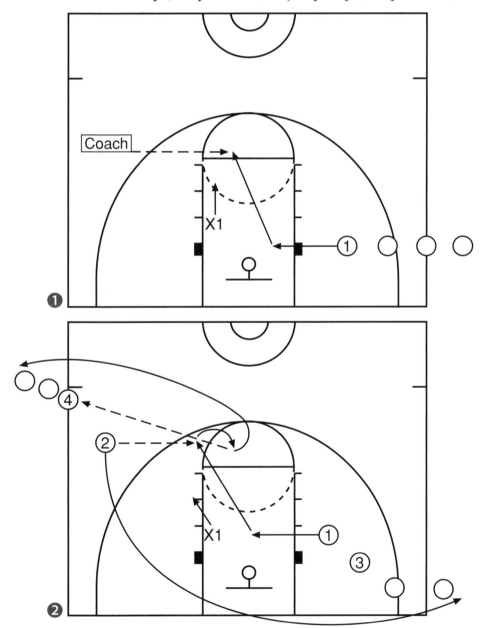

Related Drills: 38, 40, 47-49, 51-53, 55-58, 90-95

51 Flash Pivot, Triple Threat, and Offensive Moves

Individual or team • 10 minutes

Skill Focus ▷ Triple-threat position (6); rocker step (8); in and out (9, 24); crossover (10, 25); spin (11, 26); half spin (12, 27); front pivot (31); reverse pivot (32); jump stop (33); stride stop (34); chest pass (38); bounce pass (38); overhead pass (38); pass receiving (38); slide step (40); fake passing (41); swim move (47); middle cut (48); back-door cut (49); flash pivot (50); pump fake (75); pump-fake crossover (75); slide dribble (76); fence slide (96); front foot to pivot foot (97); advance step (99); retreat step (99); swing step (99); close out receiver (105)

Beginner

1. Line up as shown in the diagram.
2. Player 1 flash pivot cuts, and 2 passes to 1 while X1 tries to prevent 1 from getting the pass.
3. Player 1 uses fakes designated by the coach; X1 plays front foot to pivot foot defense. Player 1 makes his moves while X1 offers token defense.
4. As 1 goes to the end of line 2, 2 goes to the end of X2's line, and X1 goes to the end of 1's line.

Intermediate

1. Instead of step 3 in the beginner procedure, X1 plays his defense and 1 must read X1's defensive techniques and use the move that counteracts X1's tactics.

Advanced

1. Execute the intermediate drill, but require that 1 do a jump stop at the end of his dribble near the basket and use a move at the end of the dribble. (Some moves he could choose include the pump fake, pump-fake crossover, spin, and half spin.)

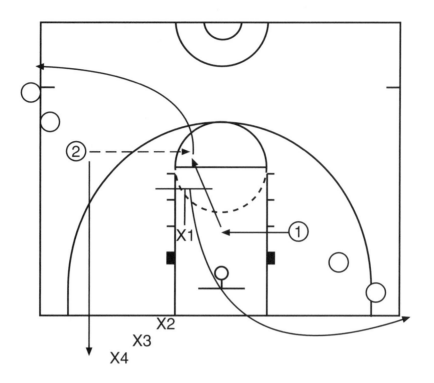

Related Drills: 6, 8-12, 24-27, 31-33, 38, 40, 41, 47-50, 52, 53, 55-58, 75, 76, 90-99, 110

52 Two-Player Cutting Drill

Team • 3 minutes

Skill Focus ▶ Triple-threat position (6); rocker step (8); in and out (9, 24); crossover (10, 25); spin (11, 26); half spin (12, 27); front pivot (31); reverse pivot (32); jump stop (33); stride stop (34); chest pass (38); bounce pass (38); overhead pass (38); pass receiving (38); slide step (40); fake passing (41); V-cut (47); middle cut (48); back-door cut (49); flash pivot (50); motion offense rules (90)

Beginner

1. Line up as shown in the diagram. In this drill, you'll begin to teach the rules of the motion offense. There is no structure for either 1 or 2. Each chooses a cut, makes it, then tells which cut he makes and the reason for the cut. Place six cones at different spots on the court from day to day. To cut between the passer and a cone is a middle cut. To cut behind a cone is a back-door cut. To replace oneself or to V-cut to any spot on the court, a player says "V-cut." Players must maintain 15-foot spacing, even if they have to dribble to do so.

2. Player 1 passes to 2 (see diagram). The following describes the action in the diagram; in your drills, it should differ from player to player and from time to time. Let the players decide.

3. Player 1 uses the middle cut, so he calls "middle cut." Reason: "Defender did not jump to the ball when I passed."

4. Player 2 sees that he is more than 15 feet away from 1, so he dribbles toward 1. Reason: "To keep proper spacing."

5. Player 2 passes to 1 and back-door cuts, so he calls out "back-door cut." Reason: "My defender overplayed the passing lane."

6. The drill continues for one minute with players making V-cuts, middle cuts, and back-door cuts, and dribbling to keep 15-foot spacing. Then players go to the end of the line while two new players come forward.

Teaching Points ▶

1. The first rule of motion offense: *Use the cut your defender gives you.*
2. The second rule: *Maintain 15-foot spacing.*
3. A player may use rocker steps and dribbling moves to drive to the basket and pass back outside. In drills, he must explain his maneuver when he makes it.

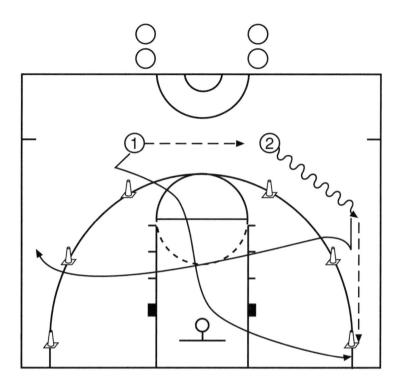

Related Drills: 6, 8-12, 24-27, 31-33, 38, 40, 41, 47-51, 53, 55-58, 75, 76, 90-95

53 Three-Player Cutting Drill

Team • 9 minutes

Skill Focus ▶ Triple-threat position (6); rocker step (8); in and out (9, 24); crossover (10, 25); spin (11, 26); half spin (12, 27); front pivot (31); reverse pivot (32); jump stop (33); stride stop (34); chest pass (38); bounce pass (38); overhead pass (38); pass receiving (38); slide step (40); fake passing (41); V-cut (47); middle cut (48); back-door cut (49); flash pivot (50); motion offense rules (90)

Beginner

1. Line up as shown in the diagram. Three-player cutting is used to teach two more rules of the motion offense to go with the two in drill 52: *Every player must move on every pass,* and *When a player dribbles toward you, you must cut or fade.*

2. The following describes the action in the diagram; in your drills, it should differ from player to player and from time to time. Let the players decide. They must tell what they did and why they did it. Five cones are used in this description, but you may use more or less. Just be sure to change the cone locations from day to day.

3. Player 2 passes to 3 and calls out "middle cut." Reason: "The defender didn't jump to the ball when I passed."

4. Meanwhile, 1 V-cuts, calling out "V-cut." Reason: "Every player must move on every pass," or "To keep 15-foot spacing."

5. Player 3 dribbles toward 1, and 1 calls out "fade." Reason: "Any dribble toward a properly spaced player, that player must cut or fade."

6. When 3 passes, 3 must tell what he did and why. And the drill continues, using the four cutting rules, dribbling, and any rocker step or dribbling move a player wishes to make.

7. One group operates for three minutes, then goes to the end of the line. Another group steps out and works for three minutes.

Teaching Points ▶

1. Remember the first two rules of motion offense: *Use the cut your defender gives you* and *Maintain 15-foot spacing.*

2. The next rules: *Every player must move on every pass,* and *When a player dribbles toward you, you must cut or fade.*

3. A player may use rocker steps and dribbling moves to drive to the basket and pass back outside. In drills, he must explain his maneuver when he makes it.

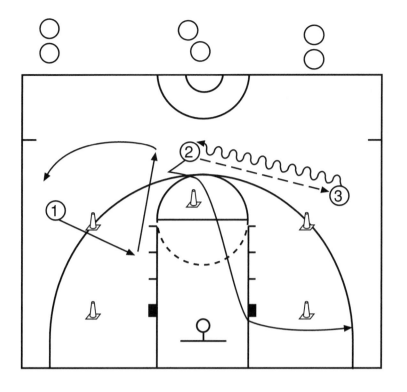

Passing and Cutting

This chapter is devoted to not only passing and cutting, but also to activating parts of the motion offense rules and to combining several different rudiments. While cuts off a pass make up the primary discussion, recognizing when to cut, when to dribble, and when to space properly receive extensive treatment.

Attackers quickly learn that they must keep 15-foot spacing. They repeatedly rehearse cuts to learn proper timing. They learn to read and react to what their defenders give them. They commit to mental and muscle memory that they must cut or fade when a dribbler moves toward them, and that they must cut every time the ball moves.

Drill 54 combines passing, dribbling, the middle cut, the back-door cut, and the V-cut. Now you are really beginning to play team basketball.

Drill 55 puts two attackers against two defenders, making it easy for the coach to see who makes mistakes in judgment, in a recognition of when to make the maneuvers as well as how to make them.

Spacing is added to passing and cutting in drill 56, as are a third attacker and a third defender. Drill 57 attaches dribbling to spacing, passing, and cutting. Again, three attackers and three defenders make it easy for the coach to see who commits errors of judgment and miscues of technique and tactics.

Drill 58 closes out the chapter with a three-on-three recognition of when as well as how to perform all the techniques and tactics of passing, dribbling, cutting, and spacing.

Two-on-Two Pass, Dribble, and Cut

Team • 3 minutes

Skill Focus ▶ Triple-threat position (6); rocker step (8); in and out (9, 24); crossover (10, 25); spin (11, 26); half spin (12, 27); front pivot (31); reverse pivot (32); jump stop (33); stride stop (34); chest pass (38); bounce pass (38); overhead pass (38); pass receiving (38); slide step (40); fake passing (41); V-cut (47); middle cut (48); back-door cut (49); motion offense rules (90)

Beginner

1. Line up as shown in figures 1, 2, and 3. Figure 1 shows the middle cut, figure 2 displays the back-door cut, and figure 3 exhibits the V-cut. In this drill, each cut needs to be run separately. The defense must simulate the coverage which activates that one particular cut. This teaches the attackers the recognition of when to run that exclusive cut. After one minute, offense rotates to defense, and defense goes to the end of the line.

2. Players 1 and 2, in each diagram, create their own cuts based on the way the defense plays them; unlike in previous drills, they do not have to explain their moves. You will notice in each instance players do not have to pass to make a cut. Players may cut any time the ball moves by pass or by dribble.

3. Player 1, in all diagrams, can use fakes, rocker step, and dribbling moves to drive to the basket, then pass back out to 2. Player 1 cuts and 2 can use his fakes, rocker step, or dribbling moves.

4. The following steps describe the action shown in figure 1; but remember, your drill sequences will be different every time, because they are based on the way play evolves. For clarity's sake, defenders are not shown following their assignments in the diagrams.

5. Defenders should drop away from their assignment instead of jumping toward the ball. This signals the middle cut (figure 1).

6. Player 2 dribbles into the frontcourt. Player 1 sees that his defender is not playing him properly, so he middle cuts. Player 2 can then hit 1 for the driving layup, and the play starts over.

7. In figure 1, 2 passes to 1 after 1 has come back out to a wing. Player 2 middle cuts; if 1 could have hit 2 for a layup, they would start over.

Back-Door Cut

Options ▶ 1. Repeat steps 1 through 3 above. Defenders should overplay between the ball and their assignment, sometimes exaggerating their knees coming over their toes. This beckons the back-door cut.

2. Player 2 dribbles into the frontcourt (figure 2). Player 1 sees that his defender is not playing him properly, so he back-door cuts. A cutter may back-door cut any time his defender overplays between the passer and the cutter; or when the cutter sees the defender's front knee going in front of his toes; or when the defender takes his eyes off the cutter to watch the ballhandler. Player 2 can hit 1 for the driving layup, and the play starts over.

3. But in figure 2, 2 passes to 1 after 1 has come back out to a wing.

4. Player 2 back-door cuts. If 1 could have hit 2 for a layup, they would have started over. But 2 cuts into the corner and his defender, X2, follows him.

V-Cut

1. Repeat steps 1 through 3 in the beginner drill. When defenders play proper denial defense, middle and back-door cuts are not available, so V-cuts provide ways for teammates to reverse the ball even under pressure. Remember the motion offense rule: *Every player must move on every pass;* the V-cut permits the player to follow this rule by simply replacing himself. That is the purpose of this drill: to recognize when to use the cuts as well as how to make them.
2. Player 2 dribbles into frontcourt (figure 3). Player 1 sees that he gains no advantage with a middle or back-door cut, so he V-cuts. A player may V-cut any time the ball moves by pass or by dribble. A player may V-cut to keep the 15-foot spacing required by motion offense rules. So player 1 V-cuts to replace himself; 2 hits 1 after 1 has come back out to a guard position.
3. Then 2 V-cuts toward the corner; 1 could hit 2 for a layup if X2 does not cover 2 properly.

Teaching Points ▶

1. Teach the cutting rules of motion offense: *Use the cut your defender gives you,* and *Maintain 15-foot spacing.*
2. Teach the other two motion offense rules: *Every player must move on every pass,* and *When a player dribbles toward you, you must cut or fade.*
3. Players may use moves, rocker steps, and dribbling moves to drive to the basket to pass back outside.

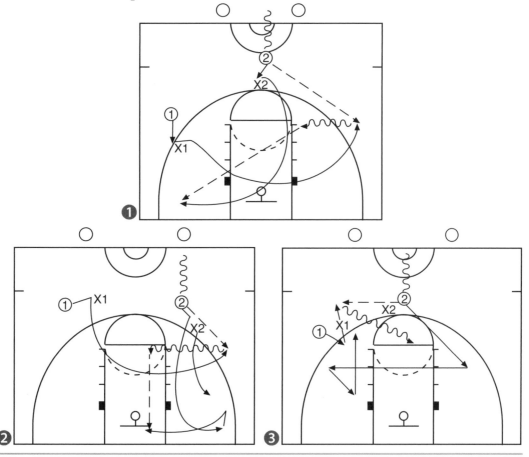

Related Drills: 6, 8-12, 24-27, 31-33, 38, 40, 41, 47-53, 55-58, 75, 76, 90-95

55 Two-on-Two Recognition

Team • 6 minutes

Skill Focus ▶ Triple threat (6); rocker step (8); in and out (9, 24); crossover (10, 25); spin (11, 26); half spin (12, 27); front pivot (31); reverse pivot (32); jump stop (33); stride stop (34); chest pass (38); bounce pass (38); overhead pass (38); pass receiving (38); slide step (40); fake passing (41); V-cut (47); middle cut (48); back-door cut (49); flash pivot cut (50); motion offense rules (90)

Intermediate

1. Line up as shown in the diagram. After two minutes, offense rotates to defense, and defense goes to the end of the line.

2. Players X1 and X2 play live defense, and 1 and 2 must take advantage of what X1 and X2 dictate. Players should have run drills 47 through 54 before using this drill. After drilling on 47 through 54, cutters will have run their cuts with no defenders, and they will have run their cuts separately with only predetermined defense. Now the cutters must recognize and react. You may run this drill before teaching man-to-man defense, but it will be more effective if you have run all your defensive drills.

3. The following steps describe the action shown in the diagram; but remember, your drill sequences will be different every time, because they are based on the way play evolves.

4. Player 2 dribbles into the frontcourt, and 1 sees X1 sagging to help on the dribbling 2. Therefore, 1 middle cuts. Player 2 does not pass 1 the ball, so 1 comes back out to the wing.

5. Now, 2 passes to 1; X2 jumps toward the pass, giving 2 the back-door cut.

6. Player 1 does not pass 2 the ball, so 2 cuts to short corner.

7. Player 1 starts to dribble outside; 2 sees this dribble and flash pivots. Then 1 passes to 2; X1 turns to look at this pass, and 1 races back-door.

8. Throughout this entire set of cuts, the offense is trying to score; so if a player can pass for a driving layup, he should.

9. At the end of two minutes, the coach should rotate the players and explain where any mistakes were made.

Option ▶ Players call out reasons for their moves while they are making them.

Advanced

Options ▶ 1. Limit the number of cuts and passes the offense may make before they must score. If the defense can keep the offense from scoring during that number, the teams rotate. A good number to start with is five passes. If the defense forces a turnover, the teams rotate.

2. Call for more cuts by allowing the offense to score only on layups—no jump shots.

1. Teach the cutting rules of motion offense: *Use the cut your defender gives you*, and *Maintain 15-foot spacing*.
2. Teach the other two motion offense rules: *Every player must move on every pass*, and *When a player dribbles toward you, you must cut or fade*.
3. Players may use moves, rocker steps, and dribbling moves to drive to the basket to pass back outside.

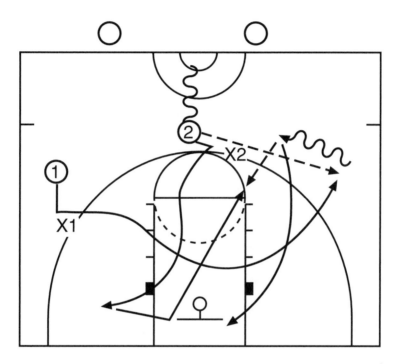

Related Drills: 6, 8-12, 24-27, 31-33, 38, 40, 41, 47-53, 56-58, 75, 76, 90-95

56 Three-on-Three Passing, Cutting, and Spacing

Team • 4 minutes

Skill Focus ▶ Chest pass (38); bounce pass (38); overhead pass (38); pass receiving (38); slide step (40); fake passing (41); V-cut (47); middle cut (48); back-door cut (49); flash pivot cut (50); motion offense rules (90)

Intermediate

1. Use three offensive and three defensive players (see diagram). For clarity's sake, defenders are not illustrated in the diagram.
2. Defenders play live defense. Offense players make the cuts dictated by the play of the defenders.
3. Do not allow dribbling in this drill; players must score by cutting, using motion offense rules.
4. After two minutes, offense and defense switch roles.
5. In the diagram, which is just one of an infinite number of sequences of cuts, 1 V-cuts to the side high post. Player 2 passes to 1 and immediately cuts back-door. Meanwhile, 3 has cut back-door on the baseline. (Remember, *every player must move on every pass.*)
6. Meanwhile, 2 has V-cut back away from the basket to a side post position. On this second pass both 1 and 3 must make another cut (not shown). This continues until the offense scores.
7. This is a live three-on-three drill with no dribbling. Each player must be aware of proper spacing (15 feet).

Options ▶
1. Designate a maximum number of passes; the offense must score or the offense changes places with the defense.
2. Require that the defense stop the offense two consecutive times before the defense rotates to offense.
3. Emphasize a certain cut by allowing points each time the offense can maneuver and get that particular cut.
4. Allow only layups—this will result in many more cuts.
5. Give the offense the ball five times, then the defense gets the ball five times. The team that scores the most in their five turns wins.

Teaching Points ▶

1. Teach the cutting rules of motion offense: *Use the cut your defender gives you,* and *Maintain 15-foot spacing.*
2. Teach this motion offense rule: *Every player must move on every pass.*

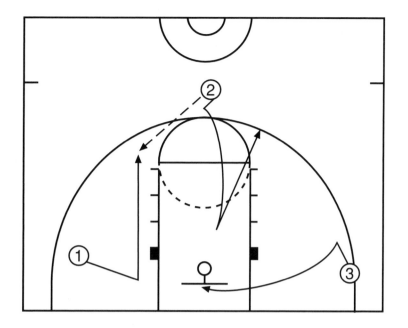

57 Three-on-Three Passing, Cutting, Dribbling, Spacing

Team • 6 minutes

Skill Focus ▶ Triple-threat position (6); rocker step (8); in and out (9, 24); crossover (10, 25); spin (11, 26); half spin (12, 27); front pivot (31); reverse pivot (32); jump stop (33); stride stop (34); chest pass (38); bounce pass (38); overhead pass (38); pass receiving (38); slide step (40); fake passing (41); swim move (47); V-cut (47); middle cut (48); back-door cut (49); flash pivot cut (50); pump fake (75); pump-fake crossover (75); motion offense rules (90)

Intermediate

1. Use three offensive and three defensive players (see diagram). Defenders are not shown in the diagram.
2. Defenders play live defense. Offensive players make the cuts dictated by the play of the defenders.
3. Dribbling is added in this drill, so the players cut, pass, and dribble, activating all the dribble moves as well as the rocker step. Players can score by cutting, faking, and driving, using the motion offense rules.
4. After three minutes the offense and defense switch roles.
5. In the diagram, which is just one of an infinite number of cut sequences, 2 dribbles toward 1, who is overplayed by X1. This is called a *dribbling entry* into the motion offense. Player 1 may fade or cut, and in this case chooses to back-door cut. If 2 can pass to 1 and 1 can get the layup, then a new sequence would begin. Player 3 V-cuts to keep 15-foot spacing, per motion offense rules.
6. In the diagram, 2 passes back to 3, which means all players must now move again, per motion offense rules. So 1 flash pivot cuts and 2 replaces himself, using the V-cut. And the moves continue.
7. This is a live three-on-three drill with dribbling. Each receiver can square up to triple-threat position when he receives the pass. Each player can drive off the rocker step or a dribbling offensive move. Moves can also be made at the end of the dribble to get off either the jump shot or the layup.

Options ▶
1. Designate a maximum number of passes; the offense must score or the offense changes places with the defense.
2. Require that the defense stop the offense two consecutive times before the defense rotates to offense.
3. Emphasize a certain cut by allowing points each time the offense can maneuver and get that particular cut.
4. Allow only layups—this will result in many more cuts.
5. Give the offense the ball five times; then the defense gets the ball five times. The team that scores the most in their five turns wins.

1. Teach the cutting rules of motion offense: *Use the cut your defender gives you,* and *Maintain 15-foot spacing.*
2. Teach the other two motion offense rules: *Every player must move on every pass,* and *When a player dribbles toward you, you must cut or fade.*
3. Players may use moves, rocker steps, and dribbling moves to drive to the basket to pass back outside.

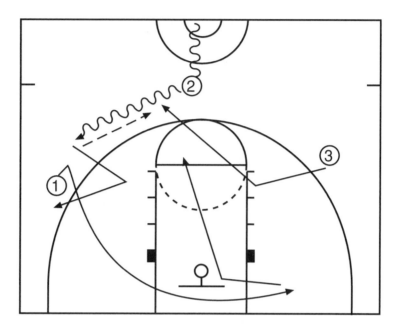

Related Drills: 6, 8-12, 24-27, 31-33, 38, 40, 41, 47-56, 58, 75, 76, 90-95

58 Three-on-Three Pass, Cut, and Recognition

Team • 6 minutes

Skill Focus ▷ Triple-threat position (6); rocker step (8); in and out (9, 24); crossover (10, 25); spin (11, 26); half spin (12, 27); front pivot (31); reverse pivot (32); jump stop (33); stride stop (34); chest pass (38); bounce pass (38); overhead pass (38); pass receiving (38); slide step (40); fake passing (41); swim move (47); V-cut (47); middle cut (48); back-door cut (49); flash pivot cut (50); pump fake (75); pump-fake crossover (75); motion offense rules (90)

Intermediate

1. Line up as shown in the diagram. After three minutes, offense and defense switch roles. For clarity's sake, defensive moves are not shown in the diagram.

2. Defenders (X1, X2, and X3) play live defense. Offense players (1, 2, and 3) must take advantage of what the defenders dictate. Players should have run drills 47 through 57 before using this drill. After drilling on 47 through 57, cutters will have run their cuts with no defenders, and they will have run their cuts separately with only predetermined defense. Now the cutters must recognize and react. You may run this drill before teaching man-to-man defense, but it will be more effective if you have run all your defensive drills.

3. For discussion's sake, we will describe what happens in the diagram. But this is only a typical sequence of cuts. Never should the same series of cuts occur again during the drilling. Let the players create, based entirely on how the defenders play them.

4. Player 1 dribbles into the frontcourt and passes to 2. Every player must move on every pass.

5. Player 1 middle cuts because his defender did not jump to the ball; 3 V-cuts to keep proper 15-foot spacing.

6. Player 2 passes to 1, who cut to the corner strong side. This again activates cuts by all players.

7. Then, 2 back-door cuts because X2 looked at the pass; 3 again V-cuts to keep proper spacing.

8. Throughout this entire sets of cuts, the offense is trying to score; if they can pass for the driving layup, they should.

9. At the end of three minutes, the coach should rotate the players and explain where any mistakes were made.

Option ▷ Players call out reasons for their moves while they are making them.

Options ▶ 1. Limit the number of cuts and passes the offense may make before they must score. If the defense can keep the offense from scoring during that number, the teams rotate. A good number to start with is five passes. If the defense forces a turnover, the teams rotate.

2. Call for more cuts by allowing the offense to score only on layups—no jump shots. Moves at the end of a dribble can be used near the basket as part of the layup.

3. Designate one player to be allowed to score, but don't let the defenders know who this player is. This compels offensive teammates to try to get that player open for the jump shot or layup. It also has the advantage of working a player who may not be as offensively advanced as his teammates.

Teaching Points ▶

1. Teach the cutting rules of motion offense: *Use the cut your defender gives you,* and *Maintain 15-foot spacing.*

2. Teach the other two motion offense rules: *Every player must move on every pass,* and *When a player dribbles toward you, you must cut or fade.*

3. Players may use moves, rocker steps, and dribbling moves to drive to the basket to pass back outside.

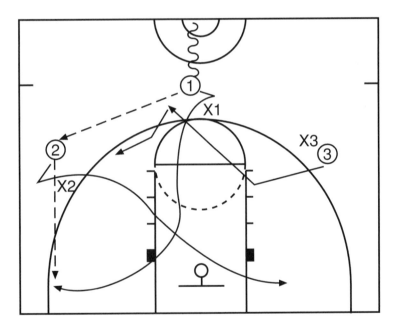

Related Drills: 6, 8-12, 24-27, 31-33, 38, 40, 41, 47-57, 75, 76, 90-95

CHAPTER

8

Screening

The purpose of this chapter is twofold: It is designed to teach proper individual screening techniques, and to add screening to the motion offense. Players should now be adept at passing, cutting, dribbling moves, the rocker step, and spacing. Add screening to that repertoire, and the motion offense becomes almost unstoppable.

This chapter, while short, builds the individual techniques and tactics of screening into a team concept. It also incorporates the screening game into the motion offense, giving the coach another offensive weapon.

Pass and screen away is covered in drill 59. You will learn how to set this screen, when to roll, when to fade, or when to replace yourself. Your teammate with the ball will learn how to determine who is the primary receiver and who is the secondary receiver. (An unmistakable key determines this.)

Drill 60 covers passing and screening on the ball. This includes the screen and roll as well as the unstoppable explosive blast. The drill illustrates how these maneuvers are added to the motion offense.

Drill 61 displays the three attackers running, running again, and running yet again all the screening techniques and tactics so the coach can determine who needs further improvement. The when as well as the how is emphasized.

Drill 62 brings all the screening techniques and strategies together in one drill. Players must learn how to cooperate to free themselves and their teammates with a screening game. Adding the screening game to your one-on-one game, your dribbling game, and your cutting game will make a formidable motion offense.

59 Pass and Screen Away

Individual or team • 10 minutes

Skill Focus ▶ Triple-threat position (6); rocker step (8); in and out (9, 24); crossover (10, 25); spin (11, 26); half spin (12, 27); control dribble (20); reverse pivot (32); jump stop (33); chest pass (38); bounce pass (38); overhead pass (38); fake passing (41); pass and screen away; screen away and roll; screen away and fade; pump fake (75); pump-fake crossover (75)

Beginner

1. Line up as shown in figure 1. Players rotate from 1 to X1 to 2 to X2 to 3 to the end of the line. Player 1 passes to 3 and goes to set a screen on X2.

2. Player 2 sets up the screen by taking a step or two away from the screen. Player 1 must set his screen on the upper half of X2's body, requiring X2 to go beneath 1's screen if X2 is to stay with 2. Then 1 rolls into the path of X2's going underneath the screen.

3. Player 2 reads X1's coverage. If X1 switches, 2 goes high for a pass from 3. Because of X1's switch, 2 is now the secondary target. Player 1 is the primary target on his roll. If 1 executed the roll correctly, X2 is behind 1 and 1 can receive the pass for a layup.

4. Player 3 reads X1's switch and passes to 1 for the layup.

5. All defensive teams teach only one coverage of the screen and roll. If you know the technique, you can predrill your squad to damage it.

6. This drill should be set up at different areas of the court each day.

Intermediate

1. Line up as shown in figure 2. Players rotate from 1 to X1 to 2 to X2 to 3 to the end of the line. Player 1 passes the ball to 3 and goes to screen X2.

2. Player 2 sets up the screen by taking a step or two away from the screen. Player 1 must set his screen on the upper half of X2's body. This requires X2 to go beneath 1's screen if X2 is to stay with 2. Player 1 rolls into the path of X2's going underneath the screen.

3. Player 2 reads X1's coverage. There is no switch. X1 opens up to let X2 slide through and keep his coverage on his assignment, 2. Player 1 rolls slightly into X2's path before breaking back toward the ball. Player 2 has a middle cut to the basket for a layup; 2 is the primary receiver and 1 is the secondary receiver.

4. Player 3 reads X1's opening maneuver and passes to 2 for the layup.

Advanced

1. Line up as shown in figure 3. Players rotate from 1 to X1 to 2 to X2 to 3 to the end of the line. Player 1 passes to 3 and goes to screen X2.

2. Player 2 sets up the screen by taking a step or two away from the screen. Player 1 must set his screen on the upper half of X2's body, which requires X2 to go beneath the screen in order to stay with 2. Then 1 rolls into the path of X2 going underneath the screen.

3. Player 2 reads X1's coverage. There is no switch. Both X1 and X2 sagged to the basket to prevent any layup, so 2 cuts toward 3 for a pass and a

possible jump shot. Player 1 fades away from the area, allowing 3 to pass to 1 for a jump shot. This fade also clears the area should X2 or X1 not close properly on 2. An improper defensive closing maneuver would permit 2 to fake and drive to the basket.

4. Player 3 reads X1 and X2's sagging techniques and passes to 2 for the jump shot or proper use of fakes.

Teaching Points ▶

1. Player 2 always sets up the screen by moving away from the place of the screen.
2. Player 1 always sets the screen on the upper half of X2's body. This compels X2 to go underneath the screen or fall behind coverage of his assignment.
3. Player 1 sets the screen as close to X2 as he can without contact.
4. Player 1 jump stops just before setting the screen.
5. Player 1 reverse pivots into X2 as he decides to go beneath the screen.
6. All offensive players, including the passer, key off X1's movement.
7. Any time a screen is set under the motion offense rules, the screener calls out the name of the teammate he intends to set the screen for.

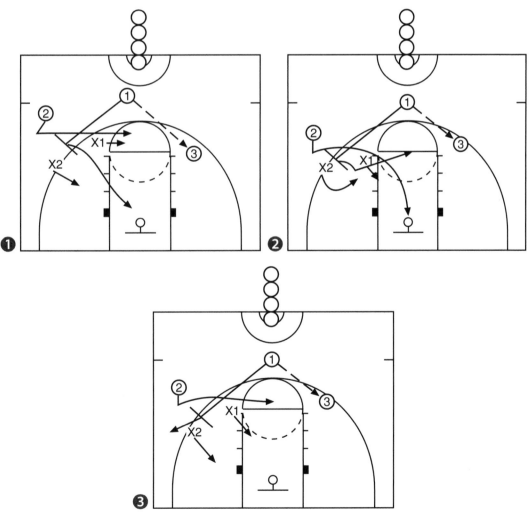

Related Drills: 60-62, 90-95

60 Pass and Screen on the Ball

Individual or team • 6 minutes

Skill Focus ▶ Control dribble (20); reverse pivot (32); jump stop (33); chest pass (38); bounce pass (38); overhead pass (38); slide steps (40); fake passing (41); pass and screen away (59); screen away and roll (59); screen away and fade (59); pump fake (75); pump-fake crossover (75)

Intermediate

1. Line up as shown in the diagram. Rotate from 1 to X1 to 2 to X2 to the end of the line.
2. Player 1 passes to 2 and goes to screen X2. (Use the same techniques as described in drill 59.)
3. Player 2 drives off the screen, looking to either drive all the way to the basket or to pass back to 1, who has rolled to the basket.
4. Player 2 drives to the basket if X2 tries to fight over the screen.
5. If there is a switch, 1 gets X2 on his back and uses slide steps to keep him there. Player 2 passes to 1 for a layup; 1 might have to use fakes at the end of a dribble to get his shot off, and 2 might have to use a fake pass to get the ball to 1. Once 1 has X2 on his back, 1 goes at least parallel to X2's line to the basket. In fact, 1 might even veer back into X2 without charging.
6. If there is a mismatch in size when X1 and X2 switch, 2 dribbles farther outside while 1 posts up.
7. There does not have to be a pass during the motion offense for a player to screen on the ball; 2 could start with the ball and 1 could come screen on the ball.
8. Player 1 must use proper talking techniques by yelling out 2's name when he goes to set the screen.

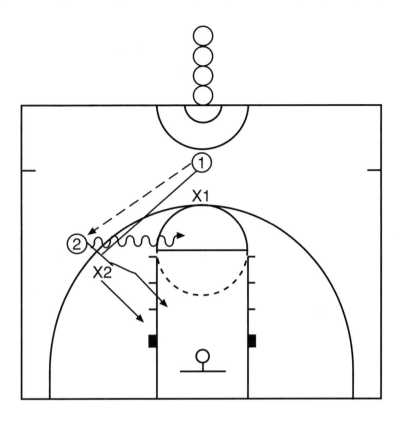

Related Drills: 59, 61, 62, 90-95

61 Three-Player Screening Drill

Team • 4 minutes

Skill Focus ▶ Front pivot (31); reverse pivot (32); jump stop (33); stride stop (34); chest pass (38); bounce pass (38); overhead pass (38); pass receiving (38); slide step (40); V-cut (47); middle cut (48); back-door cut (49); flash pivot cut (50); screen away (59); screen and roll (59); screen and fade (59); motion offense rules (90)

Beginner

1. Line up as shown in the diagram. One team runs screens for one minute or until they score a layup. That team goes to the end of the line and the next team steps out. There are no defenders in this drill.

2. No sequence of cuts or screens should be the same from group to group. Players are learning the motion offense using screens. In the diagram, 1 dribbles into the frontcourt, passes to 2, and calls out 3's name to set a screen for 3. Player 3 dips to set up the screen, then breaks off the screen but calls out a defensive switch. This tells 1 he is the primary receiver, so 1 breaks back to the ball. Player 2 passes to 1, calling out 1's name, and goes to set the screen, calling out "screen and roll." Player 1 dribbles off 2's screen while 2 rolls. Meanwhile, following the rules of the motion offense, 3 has replaced himself with a V-cut. Player 1 sees a mismatch, calls it out, and dribbles outside. Player 2 posts up the mismatch; 3, upon hearing this, flash pivot cuts to take his defender out of help position.

Teaching Points ▶

1. Remind players to call the name of the player they intend to screen for.
2. Players tell the reason they are doing what they are doing as they do it.

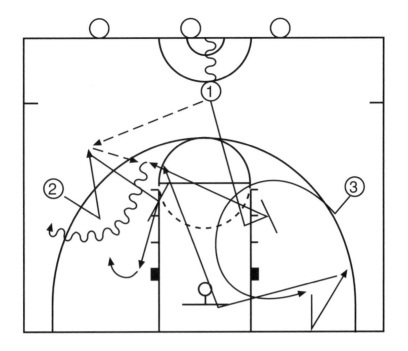

62 Three-on-Three Pass, Screen, and Recognition

Team • 4 minutes

Skill Focus ▶ Triple-threat position (6); rocker step (8); in and out (9, 24); crossover (10, 25); spin (11, 26); half spin (12, 27); control dribble (20); reverse pivot (32); jump stop (33); chest pass (38); bounce pass (38); overhead pass (38); fake passing (41); V-cut (47); middle cut (48); back-door cut (49); flash pivot cut (50); pass and screen away (59); screen away and roll (59); screen away and fade (59); pump fake (75); pump-fake crossover (75); motion offense rules (90)

Intermediate

1. Line up as shown in the diagram. For clarity's sake, defense is not shown. Defense and offense switch roles after a specified period.
2. No two sequences of cuts should ever be the same. Let the players decide what cut or screen to make and when—just follow the motion offense rules.
3. In the diagram, 1 dribbles into the frontcourt, passes to 2, and goes to screen for 2. Player 3, meanwhile, has run the V-cut, and 1 and 2 activate the screen and roll. Player 3's defender helped on 2's dribble, so 2 passed to 3 and went to screen for 1. Then 1 comes around 2's screen, and 2 thinks 1 will be open, so 2 fades instead of rolling. At that point, 3 has begun his rocker step fake.

Advanced

1. Limit the number of screens and passes the offense can make before they must score. (A good number to start with is five screens.) If the defense can keep the offense from scoring, or forces a turnover, the teams rotate.
2. Call for more screens by allowing the offense to score only on layups—no jump shots. Moves at the end of a dribble can be used near the basket as part of the layup.
3. Designate one player to be allowed to score, but don't let the defenders know who this player is. This compels offensive teammates to try to get that player open for the jump shot or layup. It also has the advantage of working a player who may not be as offensively advanced as his teammates.

Teaching Points ▶

1. Teach the cutting rules of motion offense: *Use the cut your defender gives you*, and *Maintain 15-foot spacing.*
2. Teach the other two motion offense rules: *Every player must move on every pass*, and *When a player dribbles toward you, you must cut or fade.*
3. Teach a new motion offense rule: *When setting a screen for a teammate, call out his name.*
4. Players may use moves, rocker steps, and dribbling moves to drive to the basket to pass back outside.

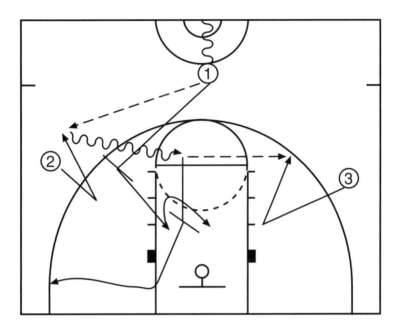

Related Drills: 6, 8-12, 24-27, 31-33, 38, 40, 41, 47-61, 75, 76, 90-95

CHAPTER

9

Rebounding

Every perfect cut, every accurate screen, every precise one-on-one move does not lead to a basket. In fact, over half of all field goal attempts are missed. Someone has to get those misses. There is a science to being in the right place when the carom comes off the board, and there is an art to keeping your opponent from that position on the floor.

First, you have to learn proper offensive footwork and how to use your hands to tip the ball until you can secure it. Drill 63 provides this instruction.

Second, you need to know proper defensive footwork that will keep your opponent from getting the perfect position on the floor—you will learn it in drill 64.

Third, you will want alternatives in case your opponent has studied your primary techniques. To progress to the next level, you'll add more offensive and defensive footwork. Furthermore, you must learn what variances occur with trajectories of the ball, shooting angles, and shot lengths. Using this knowledge, you can coax your opponent into mistakes, allowing you to get to exactly the right spot at precisely the right time. Drill 65 will reveal these techniques and strategies.

63 Tip the Ball off the Wall and Pivot

Individual • 1 minute

Skill Focus ▶ Jab step (8); reverse pivot (32); jab step and roll (65); agility; balance; quick jumping; conditioning

Beginner

1. Face a wall, holding a basketball.
2. Tip the ball off the wall five times right-handed, then catch the ball with both hands.
3. Do a complete (360-degree) turn using the left foot as the initial pivot foot. This should place you one yard or so from where you began. (It may take beginners more than two steps to do this roll; if so, let them do more steps.)
4. After completing the roll, you should again be facing the wall. Immediately tip the ball five times using your left hand. After five tips, roll 360 degrees to your right, using the right foot as the pivot foot.
5. Continue this action for one minute.

Advanced

1. Instead of tipping five times and then catching the ball, tip two times and then tip the ball a little higher and to your left one yard. Do your 360 roll, then tip the ball twice with the left hand before tipping it a yard to your right. Roll to your right and tip the ball twice with your right hand. This continues for one minute.
2. Perform step 1, but before pivoting do a jab step in the same direction as the roll.

1. To perform the roll, pivot strong on the foot in the direction you want to roll. You may even jump into the air somewhat while trying to do a twist in the air.
2. All tips should be done with the front two joints of the fingers. It should be like a catch, then a flip of the wrist.

64 Bull in the Ring

Individual or team • 4 minutes

Skill Focus ▶ Jab step (8); reverse pivot (32); swim move (47); jab step and roll (65); jab step and go (65); pump fakes (75); pump-fake crossover (75); agility; balance; quick jumping; conditioning; mental toughness

Beginner

1. Line up as shown in the diagram.
2. Players 1, 2, and 3 begin in the lane while the coach shoots the basketball.
3. The rebounder may put the carom back up, or pump fake and then shoot, or use the jab step and roll and then shoot. The other two may bump the player with the ball slightly with their bodies. If he misses, the three again fight for the rebound.
4. When a player scores three baskets, he rotates out of the lane to the end of player 4's line.
5. Player 4 steps into the lane and the drill continues. All players begin again with the total rebounds they have already scored.
6. Should a shot ricochet outside the lane, the ball is tossed to the coach and the coach shoots again.

Intermediate

1. Execute the drill as described for beginners.
2. When player 4 steps into the lane and the drill continues, all players' scores are wiped out—each begins with 0 scored rebounds.
3. Should a shot ricochet outside the lane, the ball is tossed to the coach and the coach shoots again.

Advanced

1. Instead of the coach shooting, the coach tosses the basketball to one of the three players, and the player who catches it shoots. If the shot is made, that counts as one of the three shots made to get out of the circle.

Teaching Points ▶

1. If possible, catch the rebound with both hands and shoot before landing with the basketball.
2. If catching and shooting is not possible and you are capable of tipping the ball into the basket, try to tip. Tipping should be done with the fingertips.
3. If the rebounder comes down with the basketball, he may have to use pump fakes to get the other two players off-balance before he shoots.

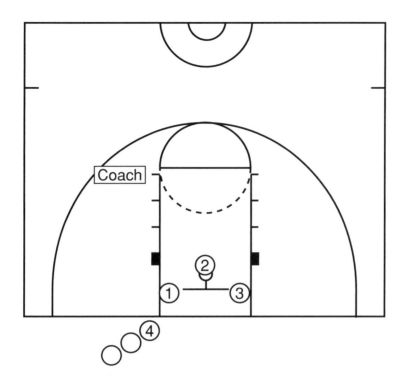

65 Jab Step and Roll

Individual or team • 2 minutes

Skill Focus ▷ Jab step (8); front pivot (31); reverse pivot (32); swim move (47); jab step and roll; jab step and go; pump fakes (75); pump-fake crossover (75); agility; balance; mental toughness

Intermediate

1. Line up as in figure 1. After one minute, offense and defense switch roles.
2. The coach lays the ball in the middle of the free throw circle. On a signal from the coach, Xs try to block the Os from getting to the ball. The Os try to touch the basketball.
3. The defense keeps the offense from getting the ball for a count of five (count "one thousand one, one thousand two . . . " and so on).
4. The defense may front pivot or reverse pivot (coach's call). Defenders may pivot immediately, or slide a step and then pivot. This is called a *defensive blockout* or *boxout*.
5. The offense uses the jab step and roll or the jab step and go; the defense will tell the offense which to use. The swim move should be used with either technique.

Advanced

Options ▷ 1. Instead of using the circle, the coach may shoot the ball at the goal. In this case, the boxouts must be held until the ball hits the floor. If an offense player gets the ball, he uses pump fakes or pump-fake crossovers to put the ball back in the basket.
2. Instead of allowing the ball to hit the floor, the defense may play it live. And if the defenders get the rebound, they can outlet pass to the coach or blast out with the dribble.

Teaching Points ▷

1. Figure 2 shows the offensive jab step, and the defensive blockout using the reverse pivot. The reverse pivot should be used when the defender is near the basket and needs to get a view of the rebound sooner; the front pivot should be used when the defender is out on the perimeter and needs to keep an eye on his assignment longer. The slide one step/pivot defensive technique is used when the attacker is an exceptional offensive rebounder. This requires the attacker to use a combination of two or more moves to get open.
2. Figure 3 adds the roll off the jab step. Because the defender blocked out, the roll was used. This enables the offensive player to get alongside the defender. The swim move should be used when the attacker gets alongside his defender.

3. Figure 4 shows the jab step and go. When the defender did not react, the attacker brought his right foot up even with his jab step (left foot). The swim move should be used as the attacker brings his right foot forward.

4. Rebounds ricochet away from where they are shot. A ball shot from the left corner will carom toward the right corner. A ball shot at a 45-degree angle will rebound at a 45-degree angle on the other side of the basket.

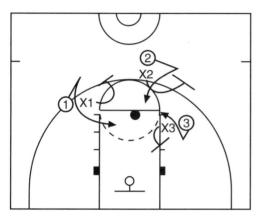

1

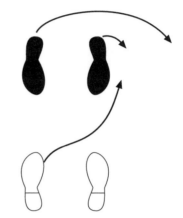

2 **Jab step** for offensive rebound. **Reverse pivot** blockout by the defender.

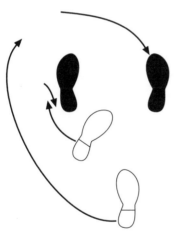

3 **Jab step and roll.** The jab step has already been completed and the defender has reverse pivoted for the blockout. As the defender completes his blockout maneuver, the attacker begins the roll.

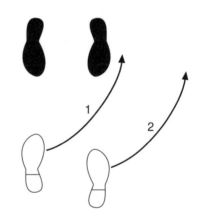

4 **Jab step and go.** The offensive rebounder has jab stepped (1). When the defender did not block out, the attacker did the go (2).

Related Drills: 8, 32, 63, 64

CHAPTER 10

Shooting

Shooting is one of the most challenging skills to master in all of sport. And once it is learned and practiced incorrectly, it is difficult if not impossible to correct. Shooting is the most difficult technique in basketball. It requires precision of muscular movement for the greatest accuracy: these activities come from the hand, the wrist, the lower arm, the upper arm, the torso, the upper leg, the lower leg, and even the toes. Your muscles must memorize these motion patterns so they can be repeated over and over again.

With so many parts of the body involved, it is easy to see how any component can get out of alignment. Hence, the *straight stick* concept is offered in this chapter so the alignment can be corrected very easily. Simply put all your elements in this straight line, and the alignment is fine tuned.

Once perfectly aligned, you must propel the ball forward and upward. *Lift, extend, flip* delivers the ball in the same manner as a catapult did in ancient times, flinging rocks at stationary targets. In this case, the basket is the target. The last shot Michael Jordan took in the NBA (as well as his first, and all in-between) was a picture-perfect *lift, extend, flip;* a model of keeping the elbow in; a flawless execution of all body parts that should be studied by aspiring shooters.

Drill 66 practices hand and wrist action. Drill 67 delivers the actual flip. Drill 68 provides the catapult step. Drill 69 combines all these ingredients in one drill. Drill 70 allows you to check alignment and thrust. Drill 71 lets you progress to a fun drill, actually using the basket as the target. Drill 72 advances you by requiring greater concentration on your shot. Drills 73 and 74 give two more practice devices to develop muscle memory for the entire process.

At any time, when either alignment or thrust becomes a problem, you can go back to the appropriate drill to correct the snag. Once righted, you can go to another drill to accelerate muscle memory learning. Younger players should use a smaller ball. Too often, young players create bad muscle memory because of a heavier basketball. Also, younger players should have the goals lowered to around eight feet.

66 Wave Bye

Individual or team • 1 minute

Skill Focus ▶ Straight stick shooting techniques (66-70)

Beginner

1. Line entire team up facing the coach, spread out about 15 feet apart.
2. Each player waves bye to the coach and holds the position after one wave. Divide the wave in two steps: *cock the wrist* and *wave bye*.
3. Repeat as many times as desired.

Teaching Points ▶

1. Hold your shooting hand up and spread the fingers until it hurts. Then relax. The position your hand naturally falls in after this is the proper shooting cup.
2. The arm should be held in front of the face, with the upper arm parallel to the floor and lower arm perpendicular to the upper arm.
3. Before players wave bye, the coach should give the command "Cock the wrist." Players hold their hand in this cocked position until coach can confirm that all have a wrinkle behind the wrist. The wrist should be cocked to a position parallel to the ground.
4. Then the coach gives the "Wave bye" command. Players hold this wave position after completion. The wrist should be straight in line with the lower and upper arm, and the arm should be extended toward the coach. The fingers should be pointing down toward the floor.

Related Drills: 67-74

67 Form Flip-Ball Drill

Individual or team • 1 minute

Skill Focus ▶ Straight stick shooting techniques (66-70)

Beginner

1. Line players up scattered around the floor about 15 feet apart.
2. Give each player a ball. Each player is to hold the ball in the shooting hand only, using only the pads and fingertips, not the palms.
3. The lower arms are perpendicular to the upper arms, and the upper arms are parallel to the floor.
4. The wrist is cocked, and the ball is in the shooting hand. The ball should be in front of the face or slightly to the shooting hand side of the face.
5. Players flip the ball very slightly into the air and catch it with only the shooting hand when it returns.
6. A piece of tape around the center of the ball makes a good shooting aid, making it easy to see whether the ball has perfect backspin. Any spinning that shows the tape whirling from side to side means the ball has not been released properly.
7. Continue for one minute.

Teaching Points ▶

1. The ball cannot stay in the hand unless the alignment is correct. If the parts of the arm are not correctly aligned, the player cannot hold the ball. It will roll off the side that is slanted or crooked.
2. The elbow must be in, otherwise the arms will be crooked and the ball will not stay in the hand.
3. If the wrist is not cocked, the ball will roll out of the hands. So the coach only needs to watch the ball to see if the alignment is correct.

Related Drills: 66, 68-74

68 Lift, Extend, Flip

Individual or team • 1 minute

Skill Focus ▶ Straight stick shooting techniques (66-70)

Beginner

1. Line players up facing each other as in the diagram.
2. Coach gives verbal cue: "lift." Players raise their upper arms to a position no greater than 45 degrees from parallel to the floor. (Do this without a basketball.)
3. Coach says "extend." Players extend their upper arms so there is very little sway at the elbow. The wrist remains cocked.
4. Coach says "flip." Players respond by waving bye and leaving palms down with fingers pointing toward the floor.
5. After repeating steps 2 through 4 several times, the coach puts cues together: "lift, extend, flip." The cues should be so close together that they sound like one word.
6. After repeating step 5 a few times, each group of players tries the drill with a basketball. One side lifts, extends, and flips the ball to the other side. The sides should be about 10 feet apart. The ball should reach its apex about two-thirds the distance from the shooter to the receiver. The ball should also be flipped at least 15 feet high. The receiver should receive the shot with both hands.
7. The shooter steps forward only slightly with the same foot as the shooting hand.

Intermediate

Option ▶ Allow the receiver to catch the ball with only his shooting hand, keeping it balanced so the ball will not fall to the floor.

Teaching Points ▶

1. Check the positions of the arm: lower arm perpendicular to the upper arm, and upper arm parallel to the floor.
2. Check to see that the wrist is cocked—there should be a wrinkle behind the wrist.
3. Be sure the ball is on the pads of the hand. Players should remember to spread and then relax the shooting hand to form the perfect cup.
4. The ball should be in front of the face or slightly to the shooting hand side.
5. Check for straight stick alignment; the ball should be in a straight line with the elbow, the knee, and the toe of the front foot.
6. Players must catapult the ball by lifting the upper arm, extending the lower arm, then flipping the wrist.

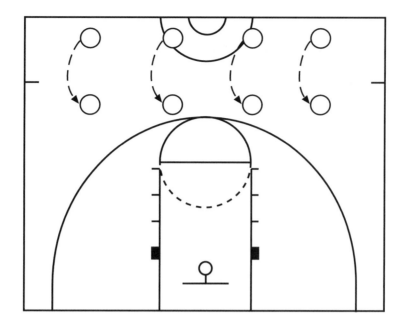

69 Lying Down Flip-Ball Drill

Individual or team • 1 minute

Skill Focus ▶ Straight stick shooting techniques (66-70)

Beginner

1. Let players lie on the floor, about 15 feet apart.
2. Each player has a basketball.
3. On command from coach, every player shoots the basketball 8 to 10 feet into the air with the lift-extend-flip technique.
4. The ball should be held directly in front of the face, with elbows in, not out to the side.
5. Players should hold the ball only in the shooting hand, but may catch the ball from its downward flight with both hands.

Intermediate

Option ▶ Execute the drill as described, but let players catch the ball from its downward flight with only the shooting hand.

Related Drills: 66-68, 70-74

70 Flip the Ball off the Wall

Individual • 1 minute

Skill Focus ▶ Straight stick shooting techniques (66-70)

Beginner

1. Player (or entire squad) stands in front of a wall.

2. For this discussion, let's let the player be a right-handed shooter. Place your right toe against the wall, with your left foot about 18 inches (or a little less) behind the right foot. Place your right knee and entire lower right arm against the wall. Cock your right wrist, with the end of the wrist against the wall. Hold a ball in the right hand. The wrist should be slightly to the right of your face with the thumb almost over the right eye. A straight line can be drawn from the wrist, down the lower arm, through the elbow, to the knee, down to the toe. This is straight stick shooting technique (figure 1), the perfect alignment for the shot.

3. Take a few steps back from the wall and shoot the ball about 10 feet into the air, letting it hit off the wall.

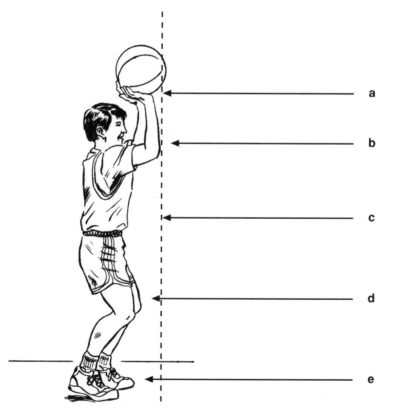

① (*a*) Wrist is cocked with ball in hand. (*b*) The elbow forms about a 90-degree angle with the forearm perpendicular to the floor and the back portion of the arm parallel to the floor. (*c*) The wrist, elbow, knee, and toes are in a straight line. (*d*) The knee is slightly bent providing balance and a leap into the air. (*e*) The toes are pointing toward the target.

continued

4. You may catch the return with both hands.

5. Step to the wall again and repeat the steps, ensuring correct alignment each time.

Intermediate

Option ▶ Execute the drill as described, but catch the return with only your shooting hand.

Teaching Points ▶

1. Check the straight stick positioning for proper alignment each time.
2. Check the lift-extend-flip techniques for proper catapulting.

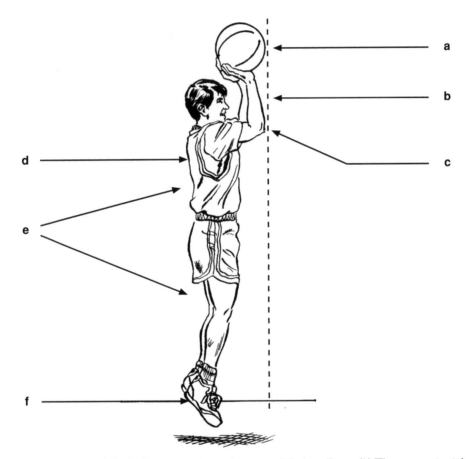

❷ (*a*) The front edge of the ball is approximately even with the elbow. (*b*) The target is sighted with the shooting eye (right eye for right-handed shooter), keeping the focus on the target, not watching the flight of the ball. (*c*) The angle of the elbow should be about 90 degrees just before lift. (*d*) Shoulders are squared to the basket. (*e*) Body is erect. Don't arch the back. Let the legs hang loose. (*f*) Let the toes point to the floor. Return to the same spot on the floor.

3. Make sure the elbow stays in throughout the entire shot. A crooked elbow is the worst fault in all of basketball.

4. Figure 1 shows proper alignment. Figure 2 demonstrates the coordination between the eyes, shoulders, elbow, and legs on the jump shot. Notice the legs go straight after the jump, and the toes point to the floor. Figure 3 displays the front view.

❸ (*a*) Wrist cocked with ball on fingertips, not palms. (*b*) Elbow should be on line to the target. Slight lateral shift of the elbow, if more comfortable, is allowed. (*c*) Opposite hand should be comfortable but lightly on the ball. (*d*) Eyes are focused on target, not on flight of the ball. (*e*) Shoulders are squared to the basket.

Related Drills: 66-69, 71-74

Around the World

Individual or team • 10 minutes

Skill Focus ▶ Straight stick shooting techniques (66-70)

Beginner

1. The player shoots from the seven spots in figure 1 and then back around. (This is called "Little Around the World.")
2. The player must make shot 1 before moving to shot 2, and so forth all the way around. When the player reaches shot 7, the coach may require the player to stop, or to go all the way back to shot 1 in reverse order—from 7 to 6, to 5, and so on.
3. The shot spot numbers are the following:
   1. Big block, left side of basket
   2. Second line, left side of basket
   3. Corner of free throw line and lane line, left side of basket
   4. Middle of free throw line
   5. Corner of free throw line and lane line, right side of basket
   6. Second line, right side of basket
   7. Big block, right side of basket
4. Players can compete against each other. The first player to complete all the shots wins the game.

Intermediate

Options ▶
1. Execute the drill as described, but allow the player to "chance" any first shot at any of the shots except 1 or 7—those must be made on the first try. Player says "chance," and if he makes the second ("chance") shot, he goes on to the next shot spot. But if he misses the "chance" shot, he returns to 1.
2. Put team A at one end of the court and team B at the other. Players on each team rotate shooting the spots. First team through wins.
3. Put team A at one end of the court and team B at the other. One player from each team tries to go around the world. Then the second player from each team tries to go around the world, and so on. The first team with a player who goes around the world wins.
4. Put team A at one end of the court and team B at the other. Each of the five players on each team is given one of the shot spots. Players shoot in order of the numbers. If a shot is missed, the player may chance it. The first team with all five players hitting from their spot wins the game.

Advanced

Options ▶
1. Add "Big Around the World" (figure 2) to the drill. Players have five new spots to shoot from (8, 9, 10, 11, and 12 in the diagram). Players may execute the drill in any of the ways that have been described.

2. Or, players may play only "Big Around the World." The shot spots are:

8. Right corner where three-point line is marked
9. At a 45-degree angle to the basket, where three-point line is marked on right side of basket
10. Top of key where three-point line is marked
11. At a 45-degree angle to the basket, where three-point line is marked on left side of basket
12. Left corner where three-point line is marked

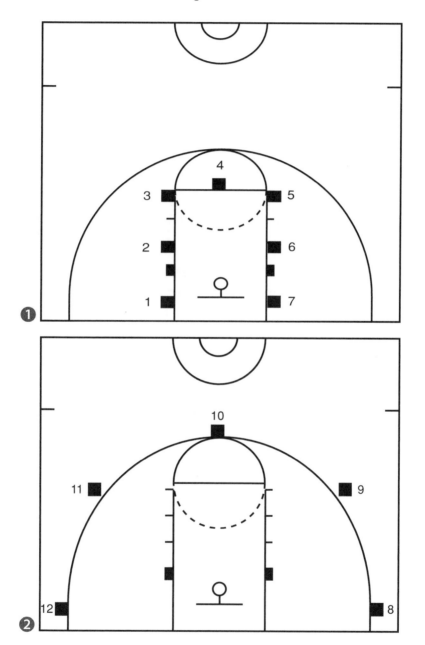

Related Drills: 66-70, 72-74

72 No Rim Drill

Individual or team • 10 minutes

Skill Focus ▶ Straight stick shooting techniques (66-70)

Beginner

1. Put two players at each basket. (If necessary, you may put four players at each basket.) Two players act as a team: one shoots and the other rebounds.
2. There are five shooting angles (see diagram):
   a. Out the left baseline
   b. 45-degree angle on the left side of the basket
   c. Up the middle of the court
   d. 45-degree angle on the right side of the basket
   e. Out the right baseline
3. Start with angle a, three feet from the basket. Shoot until you make the shot without the ball touching the rim.
4. Step back one full step, now about six feet from the basket, and shoot until you make the shot without the ball touching the rim. Continue this until you have stepped back three times. Then move to angle b, then c, and so on.
5. One player shoots and the other rebounds. Let one player complete one angle before the players switch roles.

Advanced

1. Instead of stepping back three times, step back five times. This changes the last shot of each angle from 9 feet to 15 feet.

Options ▶
(all skill levels)

1. Put teams of two against each other. They now must shoot more quickly with accuracy. First team through wins.
2. Make all shots bank shots, except the angle directly down the floor, angle c, without shots touching the rim.

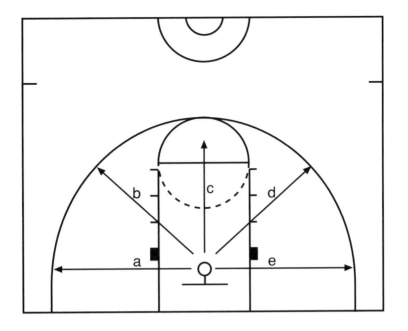

Related Drills: 66-71, 73, 74

Team • 6 minutes

Skill Focus ▶ Chest pass (38); bounce pass (38); overhead pass (38); pass receiving (38); straight stick shooting techniques (66-70)

1. Line two teams up as shown in the diagram. From day to day, change the area of the court the teams shoot from, but make sure each team shoots from equal areas. In the diagram, both teams are at the corner of the free throw line and the free throw lane line.

2. The first player in line shoots for both teams. He gets his own rebound, whether the shot is made or missed. The player then passes outside to his teammate and goes to the end of his team line. The coach may designate which pass he wants both teams to work on.

3. The second player shoots, rebounds, and passes to his teammate. This continues until one team scores 21 baskets. Teams count their score out loud as they make their baskets.

4. Teams switch places and go to 21 again so that players get practice shooting from both sides of the court.

5. If a member of team A touches team B's basketball, team B is awarded a basket. Team A is awarded a basket if team B touches team A's basketball.

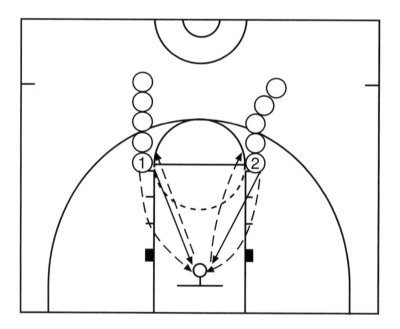

Related Drills: 38-44, 46, 52-62, 66-72, 74

74 NBA Shooting Drill

Individual • 2 minutes

Skill Focus ▶ Straight stick shooting techniques (66-70); pump fake (75); pump-fake crossover (75)

Beginner

1. A player shoots from beyond the three-point line. If made, it counts three points.
2. Whether the shot is made or missed, the player goes to get the rebound. If the ball is rebounded out on the court, the player makes a move, takes only one dribble, then shoots a jump shot. If made, it counts two points. If the shot is rebounded under the basket, the player does a pump fake or pump-fake crossover for the score. This shot counts only two points.
3. The player then goes to the free throw line. If made, it counts one point.
4. Each player is given five possessions each half. That means five three-point attempts, five short jumpers or layups, and five free throws. This gives a total of 30 points per half or 60 points for the game.
5. The goal is to score at least 50 percent of the time. Therefore, to win the game, you must score 30 points. From week to week, keep adding to the number of points you have to score to win the game. Play a regular NBA schedule, using your favorite team.

Related Drills: 66-73

CHAPTER

11

Post

There are many similarities between perimeter movement and post movement. After all, in today's motion offenses, perimeter players slide into post positions with impunity. A great one-on-one player must know how to operate in the post as well as on the perimeter.

When a perimeter player dribbling to the basket is cut off by a defender just shy of scoring and picks up his dribble, he is in the same position as a post player who has used his dribble inside. We call this *scoring at the end of the dribble.* Pump fakes are used, and the pump-fake crossover is a countermove.

A perimeter dribbler uses the spin and half-spin dribbling techniques. The same footwork is practiced by a post player with his back to the basket.

When a perimeter player squares up in triple-threat position, he uses the rocker step as his first fake. A post player can front pivot (or reverse pivot) and face the basket. We call these *face-up moves.* The face-up moves involve much the same movement as the rocker step.

The eight post drills in this chapter cover all of these techniques. These drills incorporate the defensive coverage of each move as well. That makes one-on-one play at the post very intense. Drill 75 demonstrates the fakes.

You cannot dribble outside your legs when in the post position because outside defenders sink to help force the ball back outside. A dribble outside the legs by a post player would have a sagging perimeter defender deflecting the dribble. Drill 76 will show you how to avoid this.

Drill 77 teaches fronting defense and the type of attack you need against it. Drill 78 explains the most used defensive coverage, the two-step, and the offensive tactics you must use against it. Drill 79 presents the unstoppable roll step, an offensive maneuver no post player can be without. Drill 80 illustrates the three-quarter defensive maneuver and the attack you need against it. Drill 81 practices the high-low offensive attack used by two post players cooperating against defenders. Drill 82 adds post screening as another option to your motion offense.

75 Post-Up Mechanics

Individual or team • 5 minutes per fake

Skill Focus ▶ Triple-threat position (6); rocker step (8); crossover (10, 25); spin (11, 26); half-spin (12, 27); front pivot (31); reverse pivot (32); jump stop (33); post moves; pump fake; pump-fake crossover; post-up position; drop step; face-up moves; slide step dribble (76); fronting post defense (77); one-step defensive post (78); two step defensive post (78); three-quartering defensive post (80)

Advanced

1. Line up as shown in figure 1.

2. The coach instructs players to perform a post technique. The player does the skill, then goes to the end of the line. Work on only one technique per day, or on two or three at one time—for example, post-up position, drop step, then pump fake for a layup. The following steps explain different post techniques.

3. *Posting up:* Coach tells player he is defended on the upper side. He uses his body to push his defender a step up from the big block. Coach passes inside and the player uses his drop step technique (see step 4) to score. If defender plays low side, player pushes defender a step or so lower. If fronted, the defender is pushed outside a step or two by the attacker. The body push creates a greater area for the pass. If the defender plays directly behind the post player, the post player gets low as if he were sitting in a chair and holds out his hands in front of himself for a pass. The post player keeps the defender at bay by keeping his tail protruding out back into the defender.

4. *Drop step:* Placing his front foot in front of the defender's front foot, the post player puts his arm in the defender's torso, bending the elbow 90 degrees. The arm keeps the defender from stepping around the front foot and intercepting a pass. When coach passes inside, the player moves his back foot toward the basket, still holding off the defender with his front foot and his arm; receives the pass; and shoots the layup, using a slide step dribble if needed (see drill 76).

5. *Pump fake:* The post player (who must be near the basket) squares his shoulders up to the basket and, using both hands to control the ball, violently throws both arms up toward the basket. A player may pump fake up to three times, but should shoot anytime his defender leaves the floor to block the shot. Pump fakes must look like the shot. More than three would result in a three-second violation being called. A player can use the pump fake at the end of a dribble near the basket, at the end of a post move near the basket, or after getting an offensive rebound.

6. *Pump-fake crossover:* When the defender reacts to the pump fake by coming up on his toes, the post player then uses the crossover move to step by his defender for the layup. It is important to always end the post move or dribble with a jump stop in order to have two pivot feet, enabling you to crossover in either direction. Instead of pump-fake crossover, you may use the pump-fake direct step, called the *up and under*. Use whichever maneuver your defender gives you.

7. *Face-up moves:* A post player front pivots or reverse pivots, ending up facing the basket. Now the attacker can jump shoot immediately, or pump fake then shoot, or use the rocker step to drive directly or to crossover drive.

8. *Spin move:* Same as the dribbling spin move, just performed by a post player with his back to the basket.

9. *Half-spin move:* Same as the dribbling half-spin move, just performed by a post player with his back to the basket.

Options ▶ 1. Put one defender on the post player and let the post player react to the way the defender is playing him.

2. Put an offensive player at the free throw line extended and another player in the corner (see figure 2; rotate from 1 to 2 to 5 to X5 to end of line). These two players pass the ball back and forth until the post player is able to free himself for a pass from a perimeter player. X5 can front, use the one-step defensive technique or the two-step tactic, or play behind the attacker. The offensive post player must read and react to the defender.

Teaching Point ▶

Make sure all mechanics, including footwork, are performed properly.

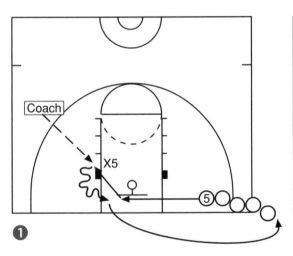

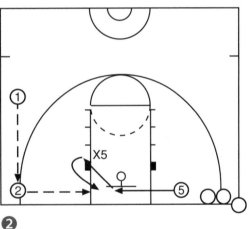

Related Drills: 76-82

76 Slide Step Dribble

Individual or team • 1 minute

Skill Focus ▷ Slide step dribble

Beginner

1. Line up as shown in the diagram. The first player in line does a single slide step dribble—one step. This step will end up at the second line marking on the free throw lane line. The player picks up the dribble. Now he does one slide step dribble to the middle of the lane. He picks up the ball with both hands, then does another slide step dribble, which should take him out of the lane. He again picks up the ball with both hands and then does one more slide step dribble, which should put him at the big block on the opposite lane. The player goes to the end of the line.

2. In the post, a player must dribble sparingly. The proper dribble is the slide step dribble. Dribble the ball no higher than the knees. Make one dribble, let's say to the right, by using the left hand, keeping the ball low and directly beneath your crouch. Slide step to the right. To do the slide step, pick up the right foot, step once, then bring the left foot up to shoulder-width apart. Keep the ball low and between the legs so it cannot be slapped away. Never dribble more than one step in the post area.

3. Practice going to the right one day, and to the left the next.

Advanced

1. After each slide step dribble, do a move, including the pump-fake series: pump fake, pump-fake crossover, up and under.

Teaching Point ▷

Make sure the dribble is directly between the legs, not out in front of them.

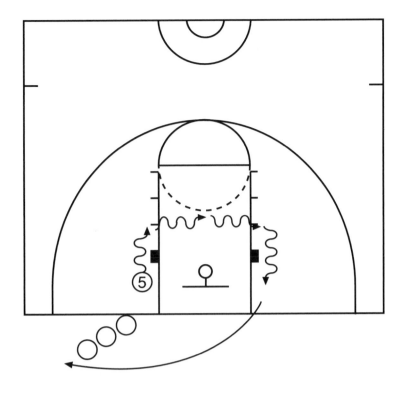

77 Fronting

Individual or team • *2 minutes*

Skill Focus ▶ Overhead flip pass (38); flash pivot cut (50); post-up offense (75); pump fake (75); fronting post defense

Intermediate

1. Line up as shown in the diagram. Rotate from offense, 5, to defense, X5, to end of 3's line; and 3 to end of 5's line.
2. Player 5 flash pivots to the big block or slightly above. X5 fronts 5.
3. Then 5 uses his body to push X5 a step or so farther outside, but not so far that X5 moves behind 5.
4. Player 5 turns to face the baseline, placing his right arm against X5's lower back; 5's upper arm should be at 90-degree angle with his lower arm. He raises his left arm and hand high over his head, giving 3 a target to throw the lob overhead pass to. Player 5 waits until the pass is directly over his head, then steps forward once toward the basket, catches the ball, and—without bringing the ball down—leaps toward the basket and lays the ball in.
5. Player 3 throws an overhead flip pass to 5. The pass should be about a step farther than where 5 has his target hand.
6. If 5 needs to reestablish his footwork, he can bring the ball down, then pump fake, then lay the ball in.
7. X5 jumps back toward the basket when he sees the ball being thrown over his head. X5 is behind the attacker, so he must time his jump to try to block the layup. X5 does not want to foul.

Teaching Points ▶

1. Make sure the pass is properly thrown—a semi-lob just slightly out of the reach of a great jumping defender.
2. The attacker should face out of bounds, and the step should be taken with the lead foot first—left foot in the diagram.
3. The attacker should not bring the ball down. Make it a catch, keep the ball up high, then lay it in.

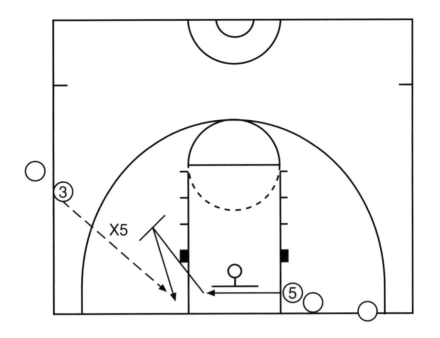

78 Two-Step Drill

Individual or team • 5 minutes

Skill Focus ▶ Triple-threat position (6); rocker step (8); crossover (10, 25); spin (11, 26); front pivot (31); reverse pivot (32); jump stop (33); flash pivot cut (50); post moves (75); pump fake (75); pump-fake crossover (75); post-up position (75); drop step (75); face-up moves (75); slide step dribble (76); two-step defensive post

Intermediate

1. Line up as shown in the diagram. Rotate from offense, 5, to defense, X5, to 1 to 3 to end of line.

2. Player 5 flash pivots to the big block area. X5 begins by playing above 5 because the ball is in 1's hands.

3. Player 1 passes to 3, and 5 tries to prevent X5 from doing the defensive two-step. Player 5 should have his front foot (right foot in the diagram) even with or above X5's right foot. X5 should have his right foot half a body above 5 and his left foot slightly below 5's body. This should become a legal pushing match, with neither the offense nor defense using hands and arms.

4. When the pass is made from 1 to 3, X5 picks up his left foot and places it directly in front of 5's body. As the pass is caught by 3, X5 should be picking up his right foot and placing it slightly behind 5's body. X5's left foot should be half a body length above 5's body. Player 5 now should be trying to put his left foot up by X5's left foot, using his lower arm to establish proper post-up position.

5. Begin the drill with 5 being inactive and X5 just drilling on his two-step maneuver. Players 1 and 3 should hold each pass about two seconds while drilling on the two-step maneuver. Then you make it live.

Option ▶ Instead of the defender doing a two-step drill, he does a one-step drill. As the ball is passed from 1 to 3, X5 pulls his left foot up and places it in front of 5's body. X5's shoulders should now be parallel to the passing line between 1 and 3. X5 keeps his hands down and reaches back to feel the movement of 5. This puts X5 in a fronting position instead of a three-quarter position. When using the one-step technique, X5 would play three-quarters when the ball is in 1's hands and fronting when the ball is in 3's hands.

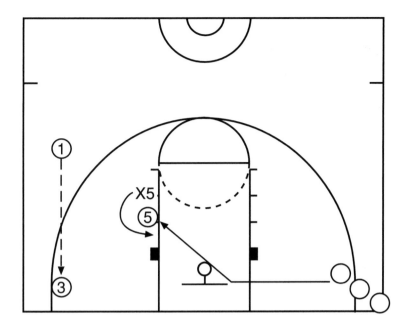

79 Roll Step

Individual or team • 5 minutes

Skill Focus ▶ Triple-threat position (6); rocker step (8); crossover (10, 25); spin (11, 26); front pivot (31); reverse pivot (32); jump stop (33); post moves (75); pump fake (75); pump-fake crossover (75); post-up position (75); drop step (75); face-up moves (75); slide step dribble (76); defensive fronting (77); defensive two-step (78); offensive post roll step

Advanced

1. Line up as if you were doing drill 78 (figure 1). Rotation is the same as in drill 78.

2. Instead of trying to prevent the post defender from moving as the pass is thrown from 1 to 3, the post player allows the defensive two-step (or one-step) movement without interference. As the defender moves, the attacker turns to face his defender (figure 2). As 3 catches the ball, the post player does a reverse pivot. Now the defender cannot possibly recover. A quick pass back to 1 from 3 gives 1 a perfect passing angle into the post. And the post player is prepared to do his offensive moves.

Option ▶ Make it a live one-on-one drill with defender and post attacker having to read and react to the developing situations.

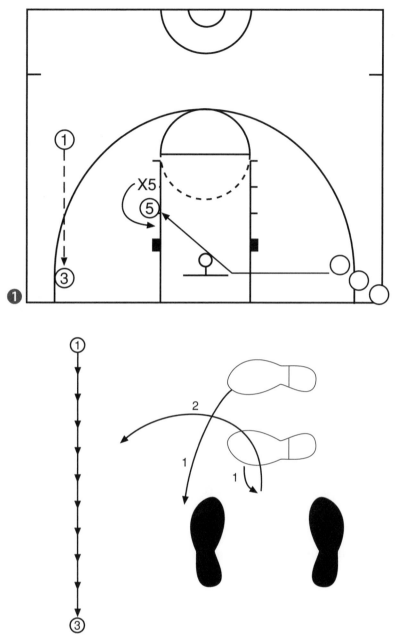

2 The unstoppable roll. Post defender does his two-step maneuver (or one-step maneuver) as pass goes from player 1 to player 3. As defender completes his maneuver, post attacker does a 180-degree reverse pivot. First step is with the foot away from the defender (right foot here) and the second step is the reverse pivot. 3 quickly passes back to 1, and the post defender cannot keep the pass from going into the post.

Related Drills: 75-78, 80-82

80 Three-Quarter Drill

Individual or team • 5 minutes

Skill Focus ▶ Triple-threat position (6); rocker step (8); crossover (10, 25); spin (11, 26); front pivot (31); reverse pivot (32); jump stop (33); post moves (75); pump fake (75); pump-fake crossover (75); post-up position (75); drop step (75); face-up moves (75); slide step dribble (76); defensive fronting (77); defensive two-step (78); offensive post roll step (79)

Intermediate

1. Line up as shown in the diagram. Rotate from 5 to X5 to 3 to the end of the line.
2. Player 5 flash pivots toward the coach. X5 defends from the three-quarter defensive position.
3. Player 5 tries to get his right foot ahead of X5's. X5 tries to keep his right foot in front of 5's. Both use slide steps to try to get this position on the floor. After several small steps, 5 will be out too far on the court, so X5 immediately tries to get behind 5. Then 5 tries to prevent this by sliding back toward the lane.
4. Allow this foot movement to continue until a defensive mistake is made. If X5 does manage to get behind 5, 5 should sit down in his chair, receive the pass from the coach, and make his offensive move.
5. Should no mistake be made in a reasonable amount of time, coach passes to 3. Player 5 releases toward the goal, trying to keep X5 on his back. Player 3 passes to 5, who tries to score. Player 5 may have to use his pump fakes and his slide step dribble to maintain balance.

Options ▶ 1. Use player 1 in place of the coach. Make it a live one-on-one post drill.
2. Play defenders X1 and X3 to try to prevent rapid ball movement outside while still drilling one-on-one in the post.

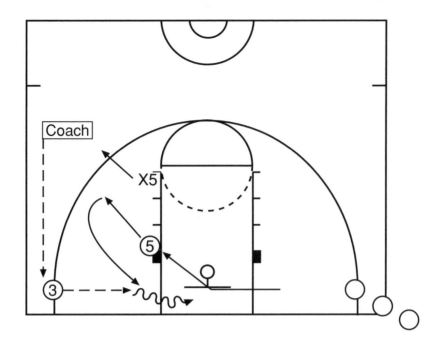

81 High-Low Post Passing

Team • 6 minutes

Skill Focus ▶ Triple-threat position (6); rocker step (8); crossover (10, 25); spin (11, 26); front pivot (31); reverse pivot (32); jump stop (33); bounce pass (38); overhead pass (38); flash pivot (50); post moves (75); pump fake (75); pump-fake crossover (75); post-up position (75); drop step (75); face-up moves (75); slide step dribble (76); defensive fronting (77)

Intermediate

1. Line up as shown in the diagram. Rotate from 4 to X4 to 5 to X5 to the end of the line.
2. Player 4 flash pivots to the free throw line area. X4 defends this move. If X4 denies, 4 cuts back-door for a lob pass from the coach. If 4 is successful in his flash pivot cut, coach passes 4 the ball and the high-low passing drill is activated.
3. When 4 receives the pass at the high post, he front pivots into triple-threat position.
4. Player 5 ducks into the lane and tries to post X5.
5. Players 4 and 5 must read X4 and X5's coverage to make the next pass. If X5 is behind 5, 4 bounce passes to 5, who uses his post moves or dribble moves. If X5 fronts 5, 4 tosses the overhead lob pass to 5 for the layup. If X5 is sealed properly, 4 steps to his right and bounce passes to 5.
6. The drill should first be done without defensive pressure. Then, after several times running the drill, the defense should become live.

Advanced

Option ▶ Put a perimeter player in the corner (or wing) on the same side as 5. When 5 seals X5, 4 could pass to the corner player, who has a perfect entry angle to 5.

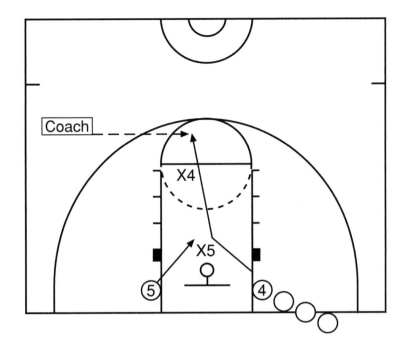

82 Post Screening

Team • 10 minutes each phase

Skill Focus ▶ Triple-threat position (6); rocker step (8); crossover (10, 25); spin (11, 26); front pivot (31); reverse pivot (32); jump stop (33); bounce pass (38); overhead pass (38); flash pivot (50); screening (59); post moves (75); pump fake (75); pump-fake crossover (75); post-up position (75); drop step (75); face-up moves (75); slide step dribble (76); defensive fronting (77); defensive two-step (78); three-quartering (80); high-low (81)

Intermediate

1. This drill consists of two phases: post screening for perimeter players (figure 1) and post screening for post players (figure 2).
2. *First phase:* Line up as shown in figure 1. Rotate from 1 to X1 to 3 to X3 to 5 to X5 to 1. Be sure to let each player operate from each spot.
3. Player 5 can screen for either 3 or 1. Both 3 and 1 must try to set their defenders up for the screen. In figure 1, 1 is setting up X1 and 5 is screening for 1. Remember, 5 must call out 1's name when he goes to set the screen and 5 must either screen and come back to the ball or screen and fade. In this case, 5 screens and comes back to the ball. The coach must read the defense of the screen so he can pass to the correct primary receiver.

Advanced

1. *Second phase:* Line up as shown in figure 2. Rotate from 4 to X4 to 5 to X5 to the end of the line. The defenders are not shown so as not to clutter the diagram. One post man screens for the other post man, and the screener rolls back high, creating a high-low passing post offense.
2. To play proper defense, X4 must always go over the top of the screen. X5 guards the big block until X4 can get there. Then X5 picks 5 back up. X5 can bump 4 slightly before going back to pick up 5.
3. The coach must read the defense of the screen so he can pass to the correct primary receiver.

Options ▶
(all skill levels)

1. Instead of the coach making the entry pass, put an offensive player there and drill on reading the screen and making the entry pass.
2. When using a perimeter player and a pass is made into the high post, 5 in figure 2, 4 can try to seal X4. You now have the high-low passing drill with a perimeter player to help pass the ball into the low post.

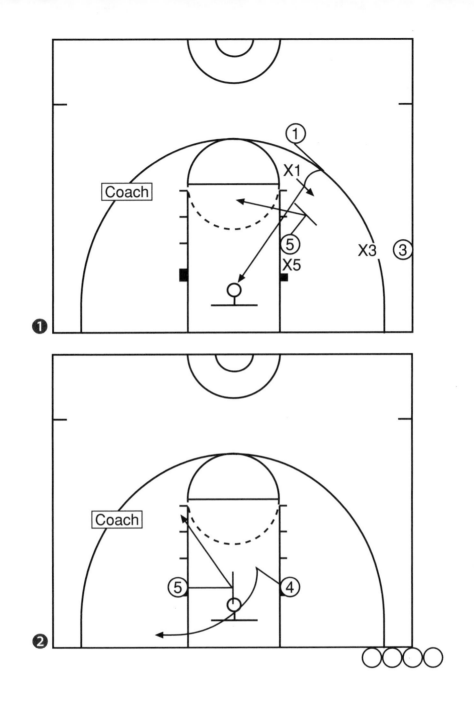

Related Drills: 59, 75-81, 106, 108-110

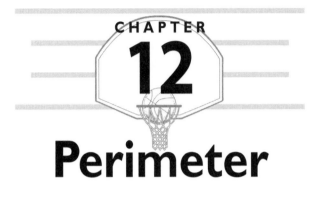

CHAPTER
12
Perimeter

Now that you have become adept at one-on-one perimeter movement without a defender, we will add a defensive player. This addition allows you to progress to knowing *when* to make a move, not just *how*. Patience is needed here, for you will make many mistakes before you become an intelligent one-on-one player. Once you have learned, you will make every player around you better.

Kobe Bryant of the Los Angeles Lakers perfected his one-on-one moves at a very young age. Today he is among the best players in basketball at creating his own shot and passing off to teammates, thereby making them better. Grant Hill of the Detroit Pistons is so smooth at his one-on-one moves that it seems the ball is an extension of his movements. Grant was from South Lakes High School in Reston, Virginia. Because South Lakes is in our area, we got to see him play before he became famous. He was smooth then; but practice, practice, practice has made his one-on-one movement flawless.

Drill 83 requires you to stay in a 15-foot lane to make your maneuvers. This is the required distance of the motion offense. Your teammates will always be cutting to keep the proper 15-foot spacing. But 15 feet is enough space if your techniques are good and you use only one or two dribbles to create separation from your defender for yourself.

In drill 84, you learn not to take a bad shot out of your one-on-one play. Drill 85 is a highly competitive, fun drill, starting with a recovery of a loose ball. Drill 86 forces constant one-on-one play.

In drill 87, you will practice never resting on the court. The bench is for resting; the court is for playing.

In drill 88, a defender masters how to close out on a one-on-one breakaway dribbler. This occurs often in a game. In drill 89, a defender learns how to close out on a weak-side pass receiver. This is the most frequent occurrence during any game.

83 One-on-One Lane Drill

Individual • 4 minutes

Skill Focus ▷ Triple-threat position (6); rocker step (8); in and out (9, 24); crossover (10, 25); spin (11, 26); half spin (12, 27); control dribble (20); defensive fakes (29); jump stop (33); stride stop (34); pump fake (75); pump-fake crossover (75); slide dribble (76); front foot to pivot foot (97); advance step (99); retreat step (99); swing step (99)

Beginner

1. Line up as in the diagram. Players 3 and X3 switch roles after a time.
2. Have several different groups going at one time at different baskets. Or you may use three groups at the same basket, each using a different 15-foot space.
3. Offense must stay inside the 15-foot lane and must score within three dribbles. Offense begins with rocker step and any dribbling move.
4. Defense tries to compel the offense to change direction as many times as possible during those three dribbles.
5. The offensive player must create separation from his defender to get his jump shot off.
6. Change the 15-foot lanes from day to day.

Options ▷ 1. Limit the offensive player to only one move (for example, spin), or two moves.
2. Instead of forcing the offensive player to change direction, the defender can play front foot to pivot foot defense and stay on the shooting shoulder.
3. Defense must stop the attacker twice in a row before rotating to offense.
4. The offensive player stays on offense as long as he creates separation, whether he scores or not.

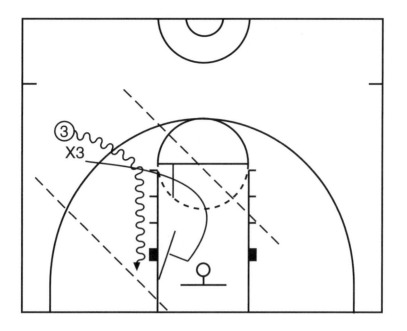

84 One-on-One Relief Drill

Individual • 4 minutes

Skill Focus ▶ Triple-threat position (6); rocker step (8); in and out (9, 24); crossover (10, 25); spin (11, 26); half spin (12, 27); control dribble (20); defensive fakes (29); jump stop (33); stride stop (34); chest pass (38); bounce pass (38); overhead pass (38); V-cut (47); middle cut (48); back-door cut (49); pump fake (75); pump-fake crossover (75); slide dribble (76); front foot to pivot foot (97); advance step (99); retreat step (99); swing step (99)

Beginner

1. Line up as in the diagram. Player 3 rotates to X3, X3 to 4, and 4 to 3.
2. Have several different groups going at one time.
3. When on offense, the player must stay inside the 15-foot lane. He may begin with a rocker step and any dribbling move. If he cannot create separation and get his shot, he is not to take a bad shot. Instead, he passes to 4 and V-cuts, middle cuts, or back-door cuts, whichever the defense gives. Player 4 hits 3 with a pass, and 3 again operates one-on-one against X3.
4. Change the 15-foot lanes from day to day.
5. The defender must play solid defense, from front foot to pivot foot to denying the shot.

Options ▶ 1. Limit the offensive player to only one move (for example, spin), or two moves.
2. The defender must stop the attacker two consecutive times before rotating.

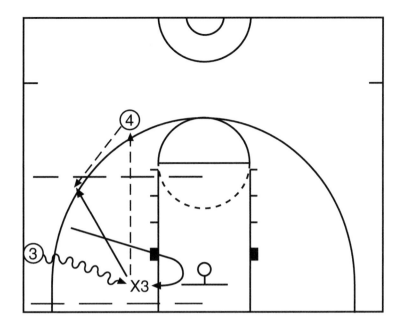

85 One-on-One Team Drill

Individual • 2 minutes

Skill Focus ▶ Triple-threat position (6); rocker step (8); in and out (9, 24); crossover (10, 25); spin (11, 26); half spin (12, 27); control dribble (20); defensive fakes (29); jump stop (33); stride stop (34); pump fake (75); pump-fake crossover (75); slide dribble (76); front foot to pivot foot (97); advance step (99); retreat step (99); swing step (99)

Beginner

1. Line up as shown in the diagram. After one minute, offense and defense switch roles.
2. Player 1 begins with a basketball and may use any fake he desires.
3. When first teaching the drill, don't let 1 dribble. Then advance to one dribble, then two dribbles. You may begin by allowing 1 to attack in only one direction, then later in both directions.
4. Player 1 may shoot when he gets X1 off-balance; he shouldn't force the shot.
5. X1 begins in front foot to pivot foot stance.
6. X1 must not leave his feet until 1 has left his.

Options ▶
1. Allow 1 to use any move, including several dribbles. X1 must react.
2. Coach stands where X1 cannot see him and holds up numbers for fakes or dribbles to be used.
3. Player 1 uses his right foot as a pivot foot one time, then the left foot as the pivot foot the next.
4. Player 1 stands under the basket and uses his pump fake and pump-fake crossover moves as if he were at the end of the dribble.

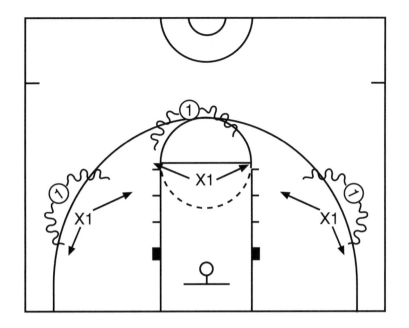

86 One on One on One on One

Team • 4 minutes

Skill Focus ▶ Triple-threat position (6); rocker step (8); in and out (9, 24); crossover (10, 25); spin (11, 26); half spin (12, 27); control dribble (20); defensive fakes (29); jump stop (33); stride stop (34); pump fake (75); pump-fake crossover (75); slide dribble (76); front foot to pivot foot (97); advance step (99); retreat step (99); swing step (99)

Beginner

1. Line up as shown in the diagram.
2. Player 1 plays one-on-one against X1, and may use any move.
3. If 1 scores, X1 goes to the end of the line while 2 comes out as the new defender on 1. If X1 stops 1 by getting a turnover or a defensive rebound, 1 goes to the end of the line and X1 becomes the new offensive player while 2 races out to defend. Whether 1 scores or X1 stops 1, the new attacker must race with the ball back to the head of the key. It is there that the new attacker reverse pivots or front pivots, establishing a pivot foot.
4. When the new attacker gets to the head of the key and pivots, he may immediately attempt a shot if the defender has not raced out there to defend.
5. A score is kept for each attacker. First player to 10 wins.

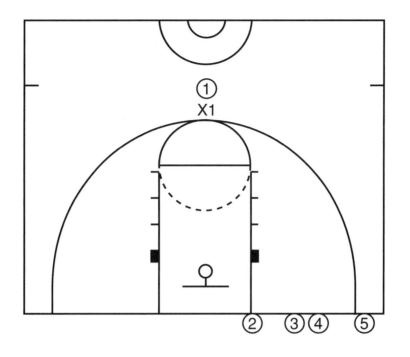

Related Drills: 6, 8-14, 75, 83-85, 87-89, 99-101, 108-110

87 One-on-One Fullcourt Game

Individual or team • 5 minutes

Skill Focus ▶ Triple-threat position (6); rocker step (8); in and out (9, 24); crossover (10, 25); spin (11, 26); half spin (12, 27); control dribble (20); defensive fakes (29); jump stop (33); stride stop (34); pump fake (75); pump-fake crossover (75); slide dribble (76); front foot to pivot foot (97); advance step (99); retreat step (99); swing step (99); conditioning

Beginner

1. This is a fun game drill. Line up as shown in the diagram.
2. Players 1 and X1 begin the drill by "throwing the ball inbounds"—to throw the ball inbounds after any score, the offensive player tosses the ball on the backboard. The two players fight for possession. The winner tries to score, and the other is the defender. In the diagram, the offensive player, 1, gains the "inbounds" pass, and takes off one-on-one fullcourt. It is best to use smaller sidecourt baskets if they are available.
3. If 1 scores, he goes to the end of the line on the side of the court where he scored. If X1 stops 1, X1 begins to drive to the far basket to score against 1. If 1 scores, X1 quickly tosses the ball off the backboard ("inbounding the ball"). X2 steps on the floor to fight for possession of this inbounded ball, and X1 and X2 go fullcourt one-on-one. This pattern continues for five minutes. The player who scores the most baskets in five minutes is the winner.
4. If you have baskets at the sidecourts, you can have two groups going at one time.

Option ▶ No substitutes. Just 1 and X1 play a fullcourt one-on-one game for two minutes. The one who has the most points after two minutes wins. Then two others go out and play fullcourt one-on-one.

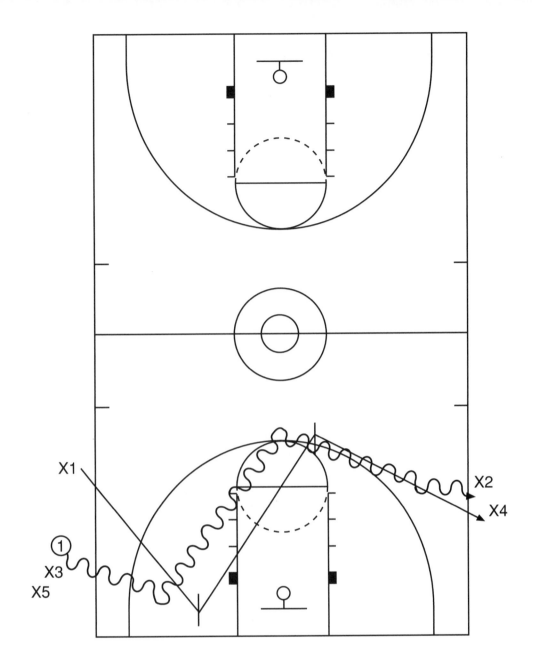

X1

X2

X4

①
X3
X5

Related Drills: 6, 8-14, 75, 83-86, 88, 89, 99-101, 108-110

88 Recovery Drill

Individual or team • 6 minutes

Skill Focus ▶ Triple-threat position (6); rocker step (8); in and out (9, 24); crossover (10, 25); spin (11, 26); half spin (12, 27); control dribble (20); defensive fakes (29); jump stop (33); stride stop (34); pump fake (75); pump-fake crossover (75); slide dribble (76); front foot to pivot foot (97); advance step (99); retreat step (99); swing step (99)

Beginner

1. Line up as shown in figure 1 or 2. These are two different types of alignments for the same drill.
2. The coach rolls the ball down the middle of the floor. He should vary the speed and distance.
3. The first two players in figure 1 race out to recover the ball. In figure 2, the coach calls out a number (in this case, 3) and those two like numbers race out to recover the ball.
4. The player who recovers the ball becomes the attacker and the other the defender. They play one-on-one back to the basket, then they go to the end of the line in figure 1 and to their former spots in figure 2.

Options ▶ 1. Make the drill highly competitive and keep the score to a certain number of baskets. Put guards on one team and big men on the other, starters on one team and substitutes on the other, and so on.
2. To make this a fullcourt transition-type drill, designate the basket at the opposite end of the court as the one-on-one basket after the recovery has been made.
3. Use figure 1 and place two cones equidistant from each line somewhere on the court, like in the corners; the players have to race around those cones before going to recover the basketball.

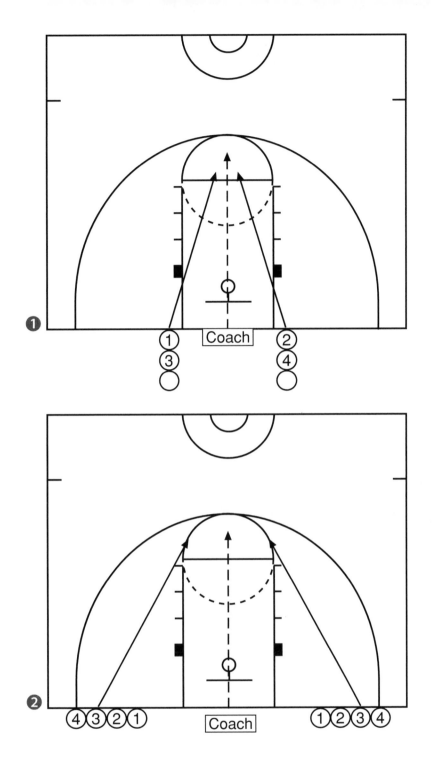

Related Drills: 6, 8-14, 75, 83-87, 89, 99-101, 108-110

89 Approach and Close Out

Individual or team • *6 minutes*

Skill Focus ▶ Triple-threat position (6); rocker step (8); in and out (9, 24); crossover (10, 25); spin (11, 26); half spin (12, 27); control dribble (20); defensive fakes (29); jump stop (33); stride stop (34); pump fake (75); pump-fake crossover (75); slide dribble (76); front foot to pivot foot (97); advance step (99); retreat step (99); swing step (99); closeout (105)

Beginner

1. Line up as shown in the diagram. Rotate from offense to defense to end of line. First player in line becomes the next attacker.
2. X1 rolls the ball to 1; 1 fakes and drives.
3. X1 must close out on the dribbler and bring him under control. Then X1 and 1 play one-on-one.

Option ▶ X1 rolls the ball to 1. X1 must get to 1 and close out on the pass receiver before 1 begins his drive.

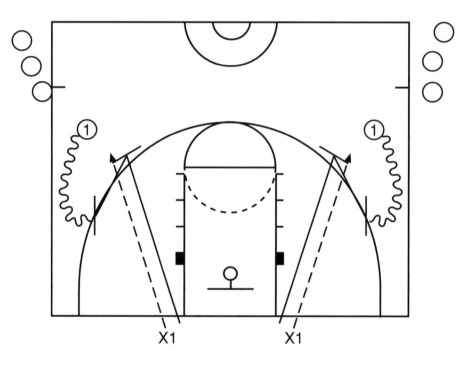

Related Drills: 6, 8-14, 75, 84-88, 99-101, 108-110

13

Team Offense

Maintain 15-foot spacing. This is rule number one for the motion offense. It not only keeps your teammates away from you while you play one-on-one, but also keeps your teammates' defenders away from you. By having a teammate only 15 feet away, you always have the option of reversing the ball.

Every player must move on every pass. This keeps the motion attackers moving; and, more important, it keeps all defenders engaged, allowing the one-on-one player to operate against only one defender.

You must use these two rules if your motion offense is to consist of just one-on-one play. This is as simple as the motion offense gets. You may add any or all of the rules listed in this chapter. The more you add, the more complicated your offense gets, and the more practice time you must devote to each option—and the harder it is for defensive teams to stop you.

Use the cut your defender gives you. By adding this to your motion offense, you have one-on-one play and cutting maneuvers. This is enough to make your club solid offensively.

When a player dribbles toward you, you must cut or fade. This allows the one-on-one player to penetrate toward a teammate and pass the ball to that teammate if your teammate's defender helps.

When setting a screen for a teammate, call out his name. This keeps your motion offense organized and allows you to add screening on the ball and screening away from the ball to the offense.

No player may stay in the post area longer than three seconds. This keeps the scoring area open for driving, cutting, screening and rolling, and post-up play.

Drill 90 activates screening on the ball for your motion offense. Drill 91 does the same for screening away from the ball. Drill 92 stresses the part of your motion offense dealing with cutting, posting up, and movement without the ball. Drill 93 gives you a chance to work on any phase or combination of movements in your motion offense. Drill 94 compels players to follow whichever rules you wish to improve. Drill 95 displays your players' knowledge of the rules of your motion offense.

90 On Ball: Screen and Roll, Screen and Fade, and Pass and Blast

Team • 10 minutes

Skill Focus ▶ Triple-threat position (6); rocker step (8); in and out (9, 24); crossover (10, 25); spin (11, 26); half spin (12, 27); control dribble (20); defensive fakes (29); jump stop (33); stride stop (34); chest pass (38); bounce pass (38); overhead pass (38); pass receiving (38); fake passing (41); V-cut (47); middle cut (48); back-door cut (49); flash pivot (50); screen away (59); screen and roll (59); screen and fade (59); pump fake (75); pump-fake crossover (75); slide dribble (76); pass and blast; motion offense; fence slide (96); front foot to pivot foot (97); advance step (99); retreat step (99); swing step (99); jump to the ball (103); deny the wing (104); closeout (105); deny flash pivot (106)

Intermediate

1. Figure 1 shows the screen and roll between 1 and 5. It shows 2 screening for 4 and fading, and 3 replacing himself with a V-cut. The defenders are left out of the drill so as not to clutter the diagram. This is a five-on-five drill following the rules of the motion offense. (For explanation of screen and roll and screen and fade, see drill 59.)

2. Figure 1 is one of many, many variations players can make up in the motion offense.

Advanced

1. The explosive blast is almost unstoppable by man-to-man defense. It is shown in figure 2, and the footwork is shown in figure 3. Rotate from 1 to 5 to the end of the line so all players will get to learn the blast from all positions.

2. Player 1 passes to 5, who has flash pivoted to the side of the key. Then 1 dips and runs directly at the left shoulder of 5. Yes, the left shoulder. In other words, 1 is going to run over 5 if 5 does not pivot. Just as 1 gets to 5, 5 reverse pivots. Now 5 can hand off to 1, if X5 stays with 5. Then 1 can drive for the layup. If X5 switches off to 1, 5 dribbles one time and lays the ball in. X1 would be on 5's back if the explosive blast has been executed properly. Player 5's read is X5. If X5 stays with 5, 5 hands off. If X5 leaves 5, 5 drives, using only one dribble.

3. Run the blast several days without defense. Then add the defense so the players can learn when to hand off and when to keep the ball. As you learn other two-player offensive tactics, you can use this drill's format to add the newly learned two-person play to your motion offense.

Options ▶
(all skill levels)

1. You can put five players on the court and run each section of this drill separately. Example: Two players will be running the screen and roll after every pass. The other three players must be screening away and replacing themselves.

2. On the next series, two players will be running the screen and fade while the other three players will be back-door cutting or middle cutting.

3. Then two players run the blast while the other three are V-cutting or screening away. These are only three of the many combinations you can drill. Don't drill any to the extent they become set plays. You want a true motion offense.

4. Run five offensive players and no defenders. Players may run any screen on the ball they wish. Players cannot try to score (you want more options run until they learn the motion offense); they must screen at different places on the court, calling out their screens as they set them.

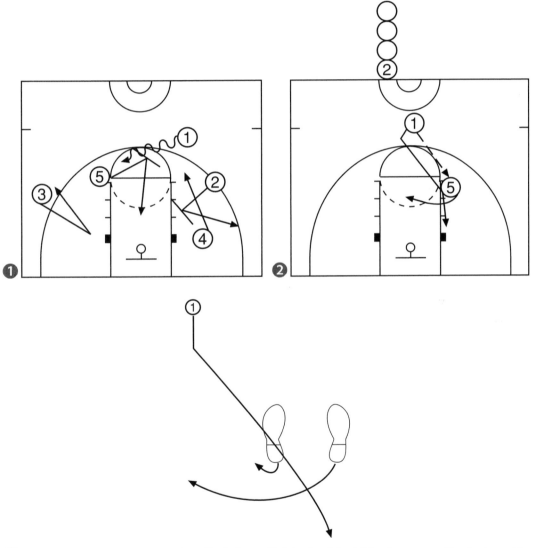

❸ The blast cut. Player 1 breaks off of player 5's left shoulder. This close cut will rub player 1's defender onto the back of player 5.

Related Drills: 6, 8-14, 59, 75, 83-89, 91-97, 99-101, 105, 108-110

91 Away From Ball: Screen and Replace or Replace Yourself

Team • 10 minutes

Skill Focus ▶ Triple-threat position (6); rocker step (8); in and out (9, 24); crossover (10, 25); spin (11, 26); half spin (12, 27); control dribble (20); defensive fakes (29); jump stop (33); stride stop (34); chest pass (38); bounce pass (38); overhead pass (38); pass receiving (38); fake passing (41); V-cut (47); middle cut (48); back-door cut (49); flash pivot (50); screen away (59); screen and roll (59); screen and fade (59); pump fake (75); pump-fake crossover (75); slide dribble (76); pass and blast (90); motion offense (90); fence slide (96); front foot to pivot foot (97); advance step (99); retreat step (99); swing step (99); jump to the ball (103); deny the wing (104); closeout (105); deny flash pivot (106)

Intermediate

1. The diagram illustrates the running of screens and the V-cut, replacing yourself. For clarity's sake, no defenders are pictured. However, this should become a five-on-five drill. Notice players in the diagram start from the same position as players in figure 1 on page 199. This is so you can see all the potential options your players can create in the motion offense.

2. Begin by running the drill without defenders. Then add the defenders. Players do not run these options from the same position on the court. Vary the positions; otherwise the players begin to make the options set plays instead of a motion offense.

3. Player 5 screens for 1 and replaces himself (see diagram); in figure 1 on page 199, 5 screened for 1 and rolled. Player 2 screens for 4 and rolls back to the ball (see diagram); 3 V-cuts, replacing himself.

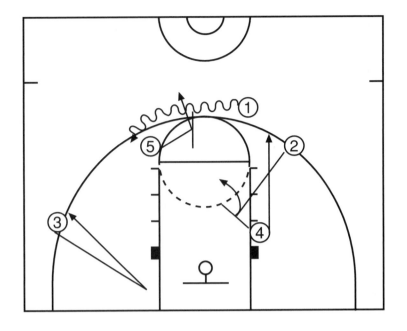

92 Three-on-Three No-Dribble Drill

Team • 5 minutes

Skill Focus ▶ Triple-threat position (6); rocker step (8); jump stop (33); stride stop (34); chest pass (38); bounce pass (38); overhead pass (38); pass receiving (38); fake passing (41); V-cut (47); middle cut (48); back-door cut (49); flash pivot (50); screen away (59); screen and roll (59); screen and fade (59); motion offense (90); fence slide (96); front foot to pivot foot (97); advance step (99); retreat step (99); swing step (99); jump to the ball (103); deny the wing (104); closeout (105); deny flash pivot (106)

Beginner

1. Begin without a defense. After several practices, add the defense. The purpose of this drill is to add the screening maneuvers to the cutting maneuvers in the motion offense. No dribbling compels the attackers to cut and to screen.

2. During the early drilling, don't let the players score. They are to just hold the ball a few seconds, then pass. After a few drills, allow scoring. On any score, teams switch roles.

3. The diagram shows 1 passing to 2 and 1 middle cutting to the basket, then to the corner. Player 3 V-cuts to the top of the key.

4. Then 2 passed to 3, and 2 set a screen for 1. Player 2 rolled, and 1 came around 2's screen for a jump shot. This is only one of many sequences the players could develop.

5. You should begin with the rule that you cannot have more than two passes without a screen being set; otherwise the players will just pass and cut instead of pass and cut and pass and screen.

Option ▶ The defensive team must stop the offensive team twice in a row before they can rotate to offense.

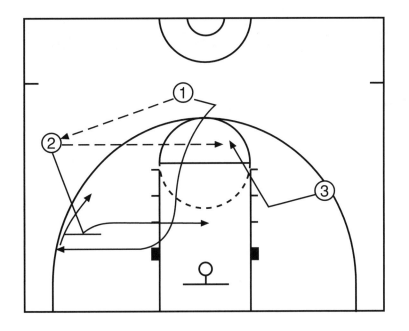

93 Three-on-Three Name Move

Team • 6 minutes

Skill Focus ▶ Triple-threat position (6); rocker step (8); in and out (9, 24); crossover (10, 25); spin (11, 26); half spin (12, 27); control dribble (20); defensive fakes (29); jump stop (33); stride stop (34); chest pass (38); bounce pass (38); overhead pass (38); pass receiving (38); fake passing (41); V-cut (47); middle cut (48); back-door cut (49); flash pivot (50); screen away (59); screen and roll (59); screen and fade (59); pump fake (75); pump-fake crossover (75); slide dribble (76); pass and blast (90); motion offense (90); fence slide (96); front foot to pivot foot (97); advance step (99); retreat step (99); swing step (99); jump to the ball (103); deny the wing (104); closeout (105); deny flash pivot (106)

Beginner

1. Line up as shown in the diagram. Rotate from offense to defense to end of line.
2. The coach huddles the three offensive players, telling them which maneuver they must run before they can score: for example, screen and roll. These tactics can be cuts, screens, individual moves (like a rocker step), and so on.
3. The coach may require players to run two distinct maneuvers before they can score.

Option ▶ Defense must stop the attackers twice before they go to the end of the line. Tell the attackers which maneuver they must run before scoring. The defense would then know that tactic for the second stopping; and the defense could attempt to stop that maneuver from being run, making offensive execution a premium.

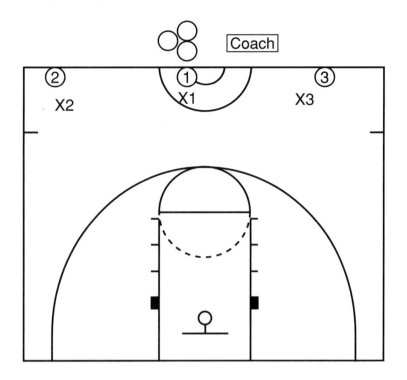

94 Follow the Rules

Team • 9 minutes

Skill Focus ▶ Triple-threat position (6); rocker step (8); in and out (9, 24); crossover (10, 25); spin (11, 26); half spin (12, 27); control dribble (20); defensive fakes (29); jump stop (33); stride stop (34); chest pass (38); bounce pass (38); overhead pass (38); pass receiving (38); fake passing (41); V-cut (47); middle cut (48); back-door cut (49); flash pivot (50); screen away (59); screen and roll (59); screen and fade (59); pump fake (75); pump-fake crossover (75); slide dribble (76); pass and blast (90); motion offense (90); fence slide (96); front foot to pivot foot (97); advance step (99); retreat step (99); swing step (99); jump to the ball (103); deny the wing (104); closeout (105); deny flash pivot (106)

Intermediate

1. Line up as shown in the diagram. Begin with no defense, then add the defense after several repetitions. Rotate from offense to defense to end of line.

2. The coach writes the six rules of the motion offense on a chalkboard in any order. Players must practice those rules in the order listed. Players may perform rule three, for example, several times before they go to rule four. But they must not call out rule five before they call out rule four. The purpose of the drill is to get the players to really learn the rules of the motion offense.

Advanced

Option ▶ Instead of listing the rules of the motion offense, the coach may list several different tactics. The offense must execute those tactics in the order listed and tell where they fit into the rules of the motion offense.

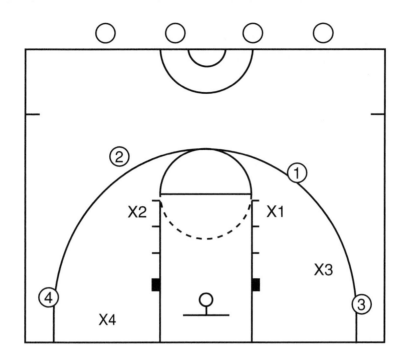

Related Drills: 6, 8, 59, 60, 75, 83-93, 95, 96, 99-101, 105, 108-110

95 Five-on-Five With No Defense

Team • 6 minutes

Skill Focus ▷ Triple-threat position (6); rocker step (8); in and out (9, 24); crossover (10, 25); spin (11, 26); half spin (12, 27); control dribble (20); defensive fakes (29); jump stop (33); stride stop (34); chest pass (38); bounce pass (38); overhead pass (38); pass receiving (38); fake passing (41); V-cut (47); middle cut (48); back-door cut (49); flash pivot (50); screen away (59); screen and roll (59); screen and fade (59); pump fake (75); pump-fake crossover (75); slide dribble (76); pass and blast (90); motion offense (90); fence slide (96); front foot to pivot foot (97); advance step (99); retreat step (99); swing step (99); jump to the ball (103); deny the wing (104); closeout (105); deny flash pivot (106)

Beginner

1. Five players begin in any formation and run the offense without scoring for a full minute. They mix up their techniques and tactics, creating new sequences at all times.

2. After one minute the team finishes with a score. The next team steps onto the floor and follows the same procedure.

3. Sequences will vary, but the diagram shows 1 passing to 2 and going to screen away for 3, then fading into the corner. Player 4 screens for 5 and rolls back to the basket. Let's say 2 passes to 5 (not shown) and runs the blast with 5. Meanwhile, 4 could V-cut to the corner and 3 could V-cut to a wing while 1 back-door or middle cuts his defender. Or 2 could replace himself while 5 and 4 play high-low. Player 3 could still V-cut to a wing and 1 could still back-door or middle cut. You get the idea.

4. This movement continues for one minute. Have teams start from different formations. The diagram starts with a 1-3-1 formation. Let the next formation be a 2-1-2, for example. Then a 1-2-2. Then 1-4, and so on.

Advanced

Option ▷ Put five defenders on the five offensive players. Start with token defense and allow the attackers to read for their cuts and other maneuvers. Then make it live five-on-five. When it is live five-on-five, the defense must stop the offense two consecutive times before they can become the offense.

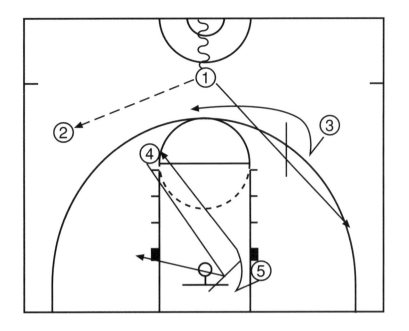

Related Drills: 6, 8, 59, 60, 75, 83-94, 96, 99-101, 105, 108-110

DEFENSIVE
SKILLS AND DRILLS

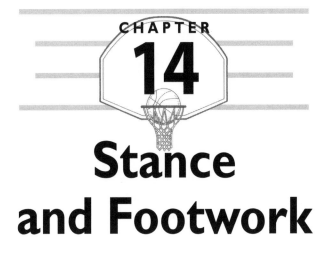

CHAPTER 14

Stance and Footwork

If you can keep your assignment from getting the basketball, he cannot score on you. In this chapter, drill 96 helps you practice this very important principle.

Once your assignment has the ball, if you can dictate where you will permit him to go, you have a leg up on eliminating his chances of scoring. Drill 97 gives you the opportunity to command your assignment to go to the spot you want him to go to.

But it is not enough for you to defend your own assignment; you must also be willing to help your teammates stop their assignments. Drill 98 gives you the opportunity to practice this all-important individual tenet of team defensive play.

Add these individual defensive rudiments to the art of stopping the dribbler (chapter 15), and you have all the ingredients to become a great defensive one-on-one player.

96 Fence Slide

Individual or team • 1 minute

Skill Focus ▷ Triple-threat position (6); rocker step (8); fence slide; front foot to pivot foot (97); advance step (99); retreat step (99); swing step (99); conditioning

Beginner

1. Line up as shown in figure 1. Rotate to the end of the line. Five new players step out.
2. Players go the length of the court and back in the fence slide position. Have players begin with left side up one time and right side up the next.

Intermediate

Options ▷ 1. Figure 2 shows the drill from a wing spot. The defender is in denial fence slide position. Player 1 uses the V-cut to get himself open. Once 1 receives the pass, he front pivots or reverse pivots into triple-threat position, then passes to the coach.

2. The coach can allow rocker step movement once 1 receives the pass, compelling X1 to use retreat step, advance step, and swing step.

Advanced

Option ▷ From triple-threat position in figure 2, 1 and X1 play one-on-one.

Teaching Points ▷

1. Let's say the right side is up. Then the right foot should be pointing straight ahead just underneath the right shoulder. The left foot should be perpendicular to the right foot with the heels of both feet in the same straight line. To get into this proper foot position, players should put their heels together at a 90-degree angle to each other, then step one full step out with the right foot. Now they are in fence step position.
2. The first step forward is with the right foot. Step out about two feet. Then bring the left heel up near the right heel. Use slide steps.
3. Your ear should be on an imaginary attacker's chest.
4. If your right foot is forward, your right arm should be extended out about shoulder high or slightly lower.
5. Your palm should be pointing outward with your thumb pointing to the floor.
6. Imagine a taut string between 1 and X1 in figure 2. When 1 steps toward X1, the string becomes loose. X1 should immediately step back to keep the string tight.
7. Once you extend the drill into the one-on-one situations, you need to review triple-threat position (6), rocker step (8), and so on for the fakes, and advance step (99), retreat step (99), and such for the defense.

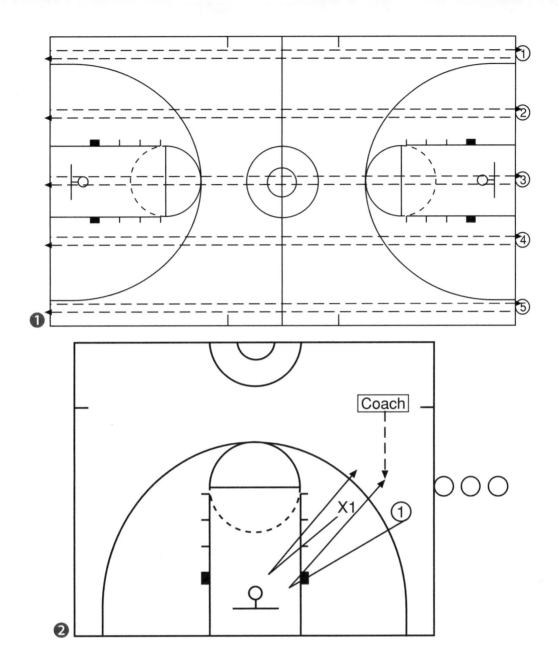

Related Drills: 102, 106, 108

97 Front Foot to Pivot Foot

Individual or team • 3 minutes

Skill Focus ▶ Triple-threat position (6); rocker step (8); reverse pivot (32); front foot to pivot foot stance; advance step (99); retreat step (99); swing step (99); slide step (99)

Intermediate

1. Line up as shown in figure 1. Make sure you can easily observe the footwork. Rotate from offense to defense to end of line.
2. Player 1 breaks to the free throw line. He is told by the coach which foot to establish as his pivot foot. X1 rolls the ball to 1. X1 must put his front foot up near 1's pivot foot.
3. Player 1 uses jab step, jab-step crossover, and reverse pivot, in that order. Observe X1's footwork.
4. Go over the drill's footwork as many times as it takes to get it perfected.

Teaching Points ▶

1. Figure 2 shows the defender's front foot up against the attacker's free foot. A simple crossover by the attacker defeats the defender.
2. Figure 3 exhibits proper front foot to pivot foot stance. On a jab step by the attacker, the defender does not need to react. He is already in a retreat step position, just close enough not to permit the uncontested jump shot. On a jab-step crossover, the defender uses the swing step. The attacker cannot shoot because his body is sideways to the basket (shoulders not square to the basket). And the attacker cannot get his front foot in front of the defender's swing step foot.
3. Figure 4 demonstrates the reverse pivot. Notice the defender uses a swing step to begin (1 in diagram). Then the defender puts his left foot up against the attacker's pivot foot (2 in diagram).
4. Under *no* circumstances would the defender ever want his front foot up against the attacker's free foot. The attacker could create separation merely by using a jab step and shooting because the defender would have to retreat a step or give the attacker a jab-step direct drive to the basket.
5. The use of front foot to pivot foot stance also gives the defender the added advantage of being on the shooting shoulder of the attacker should the attacker decide to drive toward his pivot foot, which is the only direction the attacker can go to get any type of advantage.
6. Every attacker with the ball has three things he can do: Drive away from his pivot foot, drive toward his pivot foot, or jump shoot. Front foot to pivot foot stance eliminates the jump shot and the drive away from his pivot foot because the attacker can gain no advantage with either move. The defender has dictated to the offense what the defense will allow.

7. The defender wants to be in a crouch, bending at the knees to almost a sit-down position. He should be able to touch the floor with his palms. The head is directly over his crouch and straight up, beneath the armpits of the attacker. He is bent slightly at the waist with his torso leaning slightly forward. His hands and arms should be out to both sides of his body, discouraging any offensive movement in either direction.

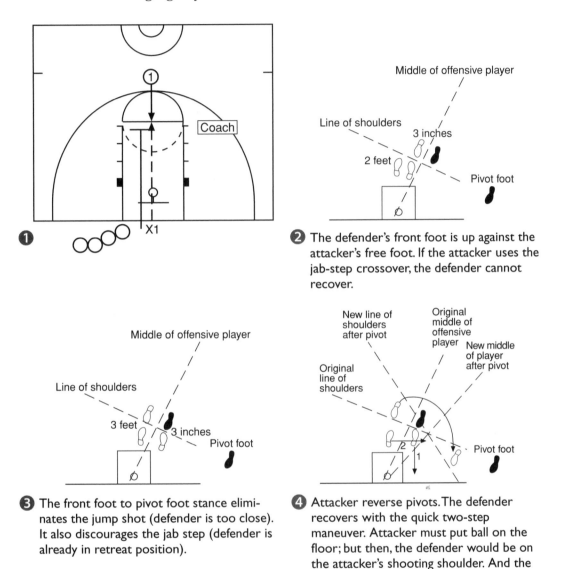

❶

❷ The defender's front foot is up against the attacker's free foot. If the attacker uses the jab-step crossover, the defender cannot recover.

❸ The front foot to pivot foot stance eliminates the jump shot (defender is too close). It also discourages the jab step (defender is already in retreat position).

❹ Attacker reverse pivots. The defender recovers with the quick two-step maneuver. Attacker must put ball on the floor; but then, the defender would be on the attacker's shooting shoulder. And the defender is back into front foot to pivot foot stance before the dribble would begin.

Related Drills: 8, 99, 105, 106, 108

98 Interception Stance

Individual or team • 3 minutes

Skill Focus ▶ Front pivot (31); back-door cut (49); fence slide (96); interception stance

Beginner

1. Line up as shown in figure 1. Rotate from 1 to X2 to 2 to end of line.
2. Player 2 uses V-cuts to make X2 use fence slides.
3. Player 1 passes toward 2. X2 pivots on his front foot and intercepts the pass.

Intermediate

1. Allow 2 to cut back-door, compelling X2 to use the other advantage of the interception stance—namely, pushing off the front foot to cover the back-door cut.

Teaching Points ▶

1. By having pressure on the front foot and being in fence slide position, a simple front pivot puts the defender in the passing lane for the interception. (See figure 2.)
2. By having pressure on the front foot and being in fence slide position, the defender picks up his back foot and slide steps with 2 on any back-door cut.
3. By being in fence slide position, 2 cannot step toward X2 and gain the advantage of the middle cut.

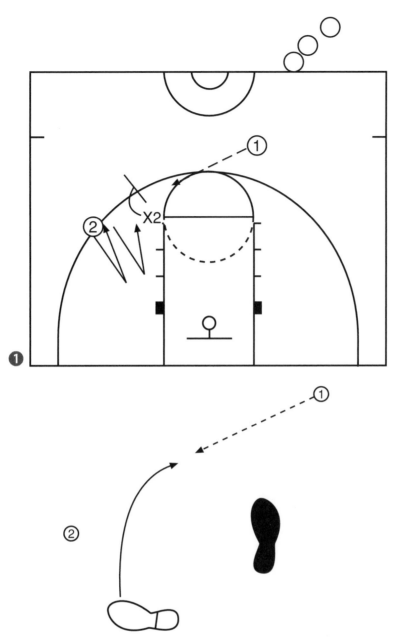

❷ Interceptor's stance. Pressure on the front foot (black) permits the defender to front pivot into the passing lane for the interception. Should player 2 elect to use the back-door cut, pressure on the front foot allows the defender to fence slide to keep player 2 from receiving the back-door pass.

Related Drills: 31, 38, 40, 49, 96, 103-108

15

Individual Movement

You should begin with front foot to pivot foot stance because you can dictate to the offense where you will allow the offense to go. However, front foot to pivot foot stance is not the only stance to begin your defense of a one-on-one player. You can play parallel. You can overplay with your front foot corresponding to your assignment's free foot. And these are only two of myriad choices.

Regardless of your beginning stance, almost all defensive coaches agree that you must master three steps to keep control of the attacker before he dribbles the basketball. They are the *advance step*, the *retreat step*, and the *swing step*, all covered in drill 99. Each of these very important steps has several drill variations devoted entirely to it. Mastery of them is a necessity for further individual development.

Once you force your assignment to begin his dribble, you will need other footwork to keep control of the attacker. You will need a slide step (drill 99). You will need to decide whether to play a parallel slide or an overplay slide (drill 100).

All this coverage will be consolidated into one coverage drill (101) for teaching purposes. Even if you are a beginning player, you should have no trouble becoming an authority at the footwork needed to dictate to your assignment. But once you have forced your assignment in the direction you want, you must *dominate* that dictation. That's where attitude comes in.

99 Defensive Step Drill

Individual • 1 minute

Skill Focus ▶ Rocker step (8); front foot to pivot foot stance (97); advance step; retreat step; swing step; slide step

Advance Step

1. Line up at the midcourt line, offense on one side of the line and defense on the other. After half a minute, offense and defense switch roles.
2. The attackers establish a pivot foot—right foot for 15 seconds, left foot for 15 seconds.
3. Attackers begin with the forward foot exaggerated forward. Defenders should be about a half step back from front foot to pivot foot stance. Attackers bring their forward foot back to a semiparallel position (the centercourt line will show this). Pivot foot should be on one side of the line and the free foot on the other side. Defenders advance step back into front foot to pivot foot stance.
4. Allow attackers to again exaggerate the front foot as if in jab-step position, and repeat the first three steps in this procedure.

Retreat Step

1. Follow steps 1 and 2 as in the advance step.
2. Defender is in front foot to pivot foot stance. Attacker jab steps, but farther away than normal from his pivot foot.
3. Defender must retreat step slightly to counter the jab step.

Swing Step

1. Follow steps 1 and 2 as in the advance step.
2. Defender begins in front foot to pivot foot stance. Attacker uses reverse pivot. The defender reacts with the one-two tactic of the swing step.

Slide Step

1. Line up as shown in the diagram. Players slide step around the court following the arrows in the diagram.
2. On each slide step, the player taps his palms on the floor. Have players always face center of court. Start from one side one day and the other side the next. Players may go around the court twice as the season progresses and they get in better shape.

Options ▶
1. When the attacker steps back into shooting position, let the shooter jump shoot. The defender must raise his arm and hand to discourage this shot.
2. Instead of going directly into the jump shot, the jump shooter pump fakes, then shoots. Defender must not react to the pump fake but must respond to the jump shot.
3. The attacker may use all phases of the rocker step and the defender must answer with intelligent defensive footwork.
4. Allow the attacker to jab step, wait a second, then dribble in the direction of the jab step. Defender must be in position to draw the charge.

5. Allow attacker to dribble a few steps to see if the defender is back in an overplay (or parallel).
6. Allow attacker to dribble a few steps, then shoot a jump shot. If defender is in proper position, he will be on the shooting shoulder of the attacker.

Teaching Points ▶

1. The defender must step forward with his front foot to the attacker's pivot foot first, then bring the trail foot back into a slightly wider base than his shoulders. The arm and hand that correspond with the front foot should be raised high to discourage the jump shot. Don't leave the floor until your assignment has left the floor on the jump shot; then put your hand between the arms of the shooter and go straight toward the ball. If you could not jump, try to cover the shooter's strong eye with your hand (usually the right eye for right-handed shooters). This completes the advance step.

2. To retreat step, the defender starts with his trail foot dropping a half step or so, then the front foot follows to maintain balance. If the attacker's jab step is away from his pivot foot, instead of forward, your retreat step should be more in that direction. Stay low, and place your arm and hand straight out in the direction of the fake.

3. As the attacker spins, the defender swings. The defender's first step is with the front foot. This step should be wider than usual, occurring just as the attacker is half through his spin move. This step should also be slightly backward because you're going to create a new front foot to pivot foot stance. The second step is to pull your former trail foot up to the attacker's pivot foot. This foot should also be slightly to the side of the attacker's other foot. The attacker cannot shoot while you swing because the attacker is sideways to the basket. This completes the swing step.

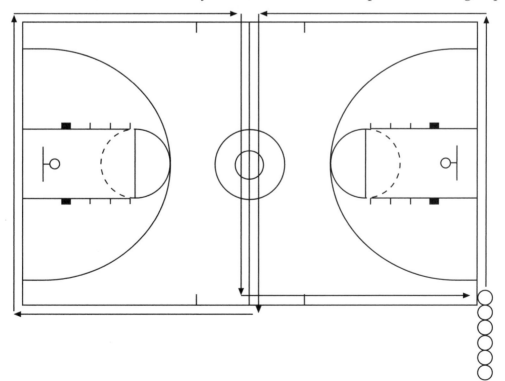

Related Drills: 97, 101, 108-110

100 Overplay Step Drill

Individual • 2 minutes

Skill Focus ▶ In and out (9, 24); crossover (10, 25); spin (11, 26); half spin (12, 27); control dribble (20); defensive fakes (29); slide step (40, 99); defensive overplay

Beginner

1. Line up as shown in the diagram. Attacker dribbles down the court and back; then the offense and defense switch roles.
2. Attackers must stay in their lane all the way down and back. Put the best dribblers in the center lane. The lane's boundaries are the sidelines and the free throw lane lines extended fullcourt.
3. Defenders must turn the opponents at least three times in each halfcourt.
4. Coach can allow the attacker to use all four dribbling moves; or the coach can drill on only a move or two by requiring those moves: for example, only the crossover and the spin move are allowed.
5. Begin by allowing the dribbler to move at a slow pace; then after several drilling attempts, permit the dribbler to try to drive by the defender.
6. At the end of the dribble the attacker must put both hands on the ball. When the defender sees both hands go on the ball, he moves in tight on his assignment.

Option ▶ Don't let the defender use his arms and hands. Make him put his arms behind his back and keep both hands in his belt. Movement of the feet then becomes a premium.

Teaching Points ▶

1. The defender keeps his nose on the basketball, meaning he is in an overplay. The dribble is out to the side of the dribbler, and the defender has his nose exactly equal to where the basketball is. Hence, the overplay is about one half of a person.
2. The defender's head should be below the dribbler's armpits. The head should not bounce up and down; it should move as though it has a bucket of water on top of it.
3. Eyes should be on the belt buckle. This part moves less than any other during a fake.
4. Slide steps should be used, and the front foot should be slightly behind being parallel to the trail foot.
5. Arms and hands should be out to the side and constantly striking in toward the dribble. These strikes should be like a quick snake strike: in and back out.
6. Defender should draw the charge if the attacker continues dribbling into the overplayed defensive body position.
7. Defender's trail hand should be down and low. This allows the defender to deflect the crossover dribble.

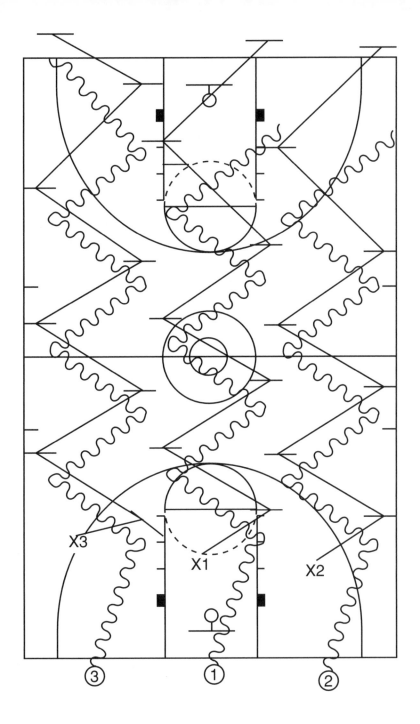

Related Drills: 101, 102, 105, 107, 108-110

101 Mirror Step Drill

Individual or team • *2 minutes*

Skill Focus ▶ Triple-threat position (6); in and out (9, 24); crossover (10, 25); spin (11, 26); half spin (12, 27); control dribble (20); slide step (40, 99); front foot to pivot foot stance (97); advance step (99); retreat step (99); swing step (99); overplay step (100)

Beginner

1. Line up as shown in the diagram. Attackers are to move parallel to the baseline.
2. Defenders are to mirror the movement of the offense by using the proper defensive step to counter the attacking move. Defenders begin in front foot to pivot foot stance.
3. Coach can call out the attacking move and watch the defender's reaction: for example, jab step is met with a defensive retreat step. Any dribble is overplayed; and when the dribbler changes direction, the defender reacts by sliding back into proper defensive overplay.
4. Begin by having an offensive move made and the defensive reaction. Analyze and discuss the move and its reaction.
5. Then permit the action to be continuous with one move following another.

Option ▶ Allow the attacker to choose the move to be used.

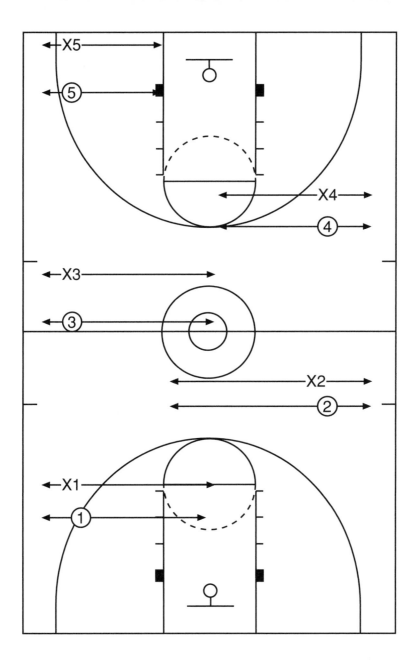

Related Drills: 100, 102, 105, 106-110

CHAPTER 16

Team Movement

Defensive team movement occurs when the ball moves (pass), when the player with the ball moves (dribble), or when your assignment moves (cut). Hence, you must know front foot to pivot foot defense to force your assignment to dribble. And you must know how to overplay your assignment so you can stop the dribbling moves. These were discussed in chapters 14 and 15. A review of these individual steps is presented in a mass drill (drill 102).

But you must know much more. You must stop your assignment from gaining an advantage by cuts and screening maneuvers. These can occur on both the strong side of the court (ball side) and the weak side (the side away from the ball). You must always know where the ball is. And you must know the rules of your man-to-man defense. Upon learning these team tactics, you can emulate Shane Battier, who played his college ball at Duke University setting all kinds of NCAA defensive records, with your defensive prowess. You can anticipate the opposition's movement and draw many, many charges.

Your first step will be to always make your assignment cut back-door. No middle cuts are allowed. You do this by jumping to the ball (drill 103); you should always be two-thirds of the distance from the ball and one-third of the distance from your assignment. And you should be one step off a line between your assignment and the ball.

On the strong side you never want a penetrating pass; therefore, you deny any vertical pass (drill 104). On the weak side, you want to offer help to your teammates, yet be in position to prevent your assignment a direct cut to the ball (drill 105). Smart teams take advantage of proper weak-side positioning. And they try to gain shooting advantages for their teammates by making you play them off their drive by one of your defensive teammates. Hence, you learn to close out on the breakaway dribbler (drill 106) and on the pass receiver (drill 107).

Then all the individual offensive and defensive techniques and tactics will have a drill so the moves will become instinctive (drill 108). Then you will be ready to move into the team defensive maneuvers.

102 Mass Wave Sliding Drill

Individual or team • 1 minute

Skill Focus ▶ Defensive fakes (29); slide step (40, 99); interception stance (44, 98); fence slide (96); front foot to pivot foot stance (97); advance step (99); retreat step (99); swing step (99); jump to the ball (103); deny the wing (104)

Beginner

1. Line up in staggered positions in the frontcourt where all can see the coach, as shown in the diagram.
2. The coach establishes a pivot foot. This should be changed from day to day.
3. All defensive players appoint the proper front foot to pivot foot.
4. The coach jab steps. Defenders react with a retreat step. Coach does a jab-step crossover; defenders react with a swing step. Coach uses spin move; defenders react with a quick one-two step, creating a new front foot to pivot foot.
5. The coach begins a dribble in one direction or the other. Players react by overplaying the dribble. Coach changes direction; players react with a retreat step with the trail foot and a quick movement into another overplay.
6. The coach picks up his dribble. When defenders see both hands go on the ball, they react with an advance step and a tight overplay.
7. The coach may have players gather in the frontcourt and run the movements again.

Option ▶ Tell the players they are on the weak side. Now you need an assistant coach to help you. In your first phase, pass the ball to your assistant coach, who is parallel to you. Defenders react by jumping to the ball. In the second phase, have your assistant move downcourt from you. Players react by denying the assistant the ball (fence slide position). In the third phase, the assistant coach moves to the weak side. Now throw a skip pass, and the players close out to the ball. In the last phase, throw a line-drive pass, and the defenders use the interception stance and intercept the pass.

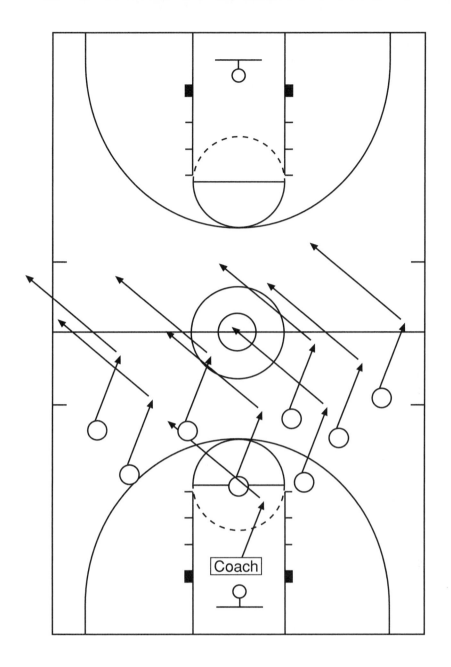

Coach

103 Jump to the Ball

Team • 5 minutes

Skill Focus ▶ Triple-threat position (6); rocker step (8); in and out (9, 24); crossover (10, 25); spin (11, 26); half spin (12, 27); front pivot (31); reverse pivot (32); jump stop (33); stride stop (34); chest pass (38); bounce pass (38); V-cut (47); back-door cut (48); pump fake (75); pump-fake crossover (75); fence slide (96); front foot to pivot foot (97); advance step (99); retreat step (99); swing step (99); jump to the ball; deny the wing (104)

Beginner

1. Line up as shown in the diagram. Rotate from offense to defense to the end of the line; the next player in each line moves out front to become the new attacker.
2. Player 1 passes to 2. X1 and X2 jump to the ball. Player 2 passes to 1. X2 and X1 again jump to the ball. This continues for several passes before rotation occurs.

Options ▶
1. The player with the ball does a jab step and jab-step crossover before passing the ball back to his teammate.
2. After several passes, the coach makes the drill live by allowing the weak-side attacker to middle cut or back-door cut into strong-side wing position. Now the defender on the wing plays denial defense. The wing V-cuts until he gets open. Then the outside attacker must jump to the ball. The wing player with the ball and his defender play one-on-one.

Teaching Points ▶

1. When each player jumps to the ball, the player on the ball plays front foot to pivot foot stance and the off-the-ball player plays in the interception stance.
2. Defenders move while the pass is in the air. Don't jump to the ball on fake passes.
3. To jump to the ball does not mean a jump off the floor. Rather, it is a quick slide step or two toward the ball with the toes grabbing at the floor.

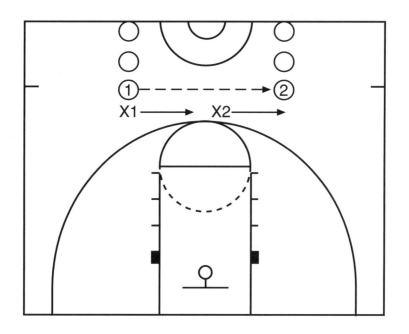

Related Drills: 96-102, 104-110

104 Deny the Wing

Team • 4 minutes

Skill Focus ▶ Triple-threat position (6); rocker step (8); in and out (9, 24); crossover (10, 25); spin (11, 26); half spin (12, 27); front pivot (31); reverse pivot (32); jump stop (33); stride stop (34); chest pass (38); bounce pass (38); V-cut (47); back-door cut (48); pump fake (75); pump-fake crossover (75); fence slide (96); front foot to pivot foot (97); advance step (99); retreat step (99); swing step (99); deny the wing

Beginner

1. Line up as shown in the diagram. Rotate from 1 to 3 to X3 to end of line.
2. Player 3 runs the V-cut. X3 denies the pass to 3. Player 3 has the option of running back-door cut if X3 makes that available.
3. Once 3 receives the ball, he front pivots (or reverse pivots) into triple-threat position. He then passes the ball back to 1, and the players rotate.

Intermediate

Option ▶ When 3 receives the pass, he front pivots into triple-threat position. Then the two players play one-on-one.

Teaching Point ▶

X3 uses the fence slide to keep the ball from 3. X3 stays one full step toward the ball from 3 but in a straight line between 3 and the ball. X3, in other words, keeps his ear on the chest of 3. X3 keeps his arm and hand in the passing lane between 1 and 3. X3 turns the palm of his hand toward 1 with his thumb pointed down. X3 uses his off arm and hand as leverage against 3. X3's off arm should be straight out into the running lane of 3. When 3 makes contact, X3 stiffens, preventing 3 from moving at full speed. X3 must not initiate the contact.

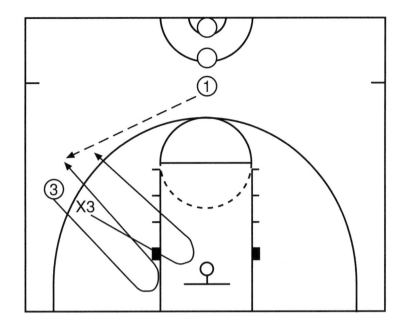

Related Drills: 6, 8-12, 24-27, 31-34, 38, 47, 49, 75, 96, 97, 99-101, 105-110

Deny the Flash Pivot

Team • 4 minutes

Skill Focus ▶ Triple-threat position (6); rocker step (8); in and out (9, 24); crossover (10, 25); spin (11, 26); half spin (12, 27); front pivot (31); reverse pivot (32); jump stop (33); stride stop (34); chest pass (38); bounce pass (38); overhead flip pass (38); V-cut (47); back-door cut (48); pump fake (75); pump-fake crossover (75); fence slide (96); front foot to pivot foot (97); advance step (99); retreat step (99); swing step (99); deny the flash pivot

Beginner

1. Line up as shown in the diagram. Rotate from 1 to X5 to 5 to the end of the line.
2. Player 5 breaks on flash pivot cut to high-post area. X5 tries to deny this cut. Player 1 passes to 5; 5 can back-door cut, and 1 can throw the overhead flip pass.
3. When 5 receives the pass, 5 front pivots (or reverse pivots) and gets in triple-threat position. He then passes to 1, and the rotation commences.

Intermediate

Option ▶ When 5 receives the pass, he front pivots and gets in triple-threat position. Then 5 and X5 play one-on-one.

Teaching Point ▶

X5 first must body check 5 as 5 cuts across the lane. This should be a full torso against torso. The defense is allowed this position as much as the offense. The defense must get there first. Then when 5 cuts up the lane, X5 uses the techniques of the deny the wing pass in drill 104.

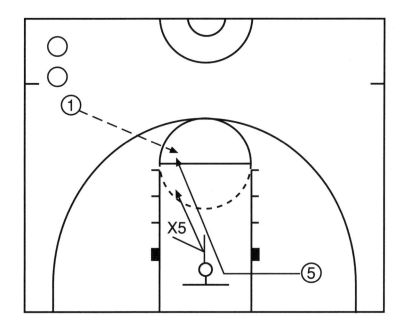

106 Dribbler Closeout

Individual or team • 1 minute

Skill Focus ▶ Speed dribble (19); control dribble (20); close out on dribbler

Beginner

1. Line up as shown in the diagram. Offense dribbles under control.
2. Defender goes to pick up dribbler and keeps dribbler under control.
3. Attacker dribbles a few steps before starting the drill again.

Intermediate

Option ▶ The offensive player uses a speed dribble. The defender still picks up the dribbler and keeps him under control.

Advanced

Option ▶ Start the drill at halfcourt and have the defender near the free throw line. When the dribbler is closed out, the two players play one-on-one at the basket.

Teaching Points ▶

1. The defender slide steps a few steps toward the dribbler. He overplays half his body so that the dribbler must change direction, either crossover move or spin move.
2. The defender uses a swing step and begins to use slide steps trying to get back into another overplay position, always keeping the dribbler in front of him.
3. This defense can occur on one's assignment or to help a teammate on a breakaway (free) dribbler.

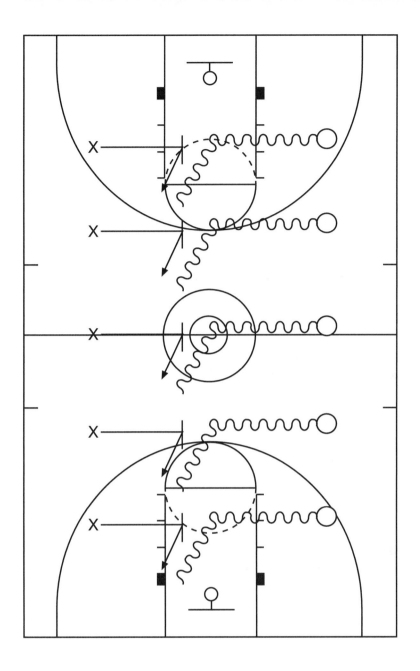

107 Skip Pass and Closeout

Team • 6 minutes

Skill Focus ▶ Triple-threat position (6); rocker step (8); in and out (9, 24); crossover (10, 25); spin (11, 26); half spin (12, 27); front pivot (31); reverse pivot (32); jump stop (33); stride stop (34); chest pass (38); bounce pass (38); interception stance (44, 98); V-cut (47); back-door cut (48); pump fake (75); pump-fake crossover (75); fence slide (96); front foot to pivot foot (97); advance step (99); retreat step (99); swing step (99); skip pass and closeout

Intermediate

1. Line up as shown in the diagram. Rotate from 1 to X3 to 3 to end of line.
2. Player 1 begins by throwing a line-drive pass, even underhanded, to 3. X3 must be in the interception stance and pick this pass off. X3 passes back to 1. Player 1 may repeat this as many times as he wishes to keep X3 honest.
3. Finally, 1 overhead lobs a pass to 3. X3 must close out on the pass receiver and keep the receiver under control.
4. Players 3 and X3 go one-on-one after a clean reception. Player 3 is allowed to move up and down the sideline, compelling X3 to continually readjust his position.

Teaching Points ▶

1. X3 is two-thirds the distance from 1 and one-third the distance from 3.
2. X3 is in the interception stance and is one step off the line between 1 and 3. He must see both 1 and 3 and must intercept any direct pass to 3.
3. To close out to a pass receiver, the defender runs straight toward the receiver, coming under control with slide steps the last few steps. He then slide steps up the straddle of the receiver, overplaying on the free foot side of the receiver. This forces the receiver to crossover or spin (slower moves than a direct drive) toward his pivot foot. The defender uses the one-two swing step maneuver (drill 97) to keep the potential dribbler under control. The defender must get to the receiver as the ball arrives.

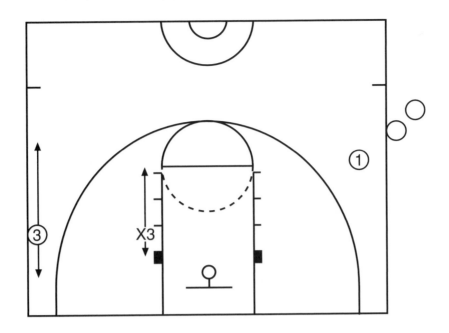

108 Eight-Point Drill

Individual or team • 10 minutes

Skill Focus ▶ Triple-threat position (6); rocker step (8); in and out (9, 24); crossover (10, 25); spin (11, 26); half spin (12, 27); front pivot (31); reverse pivot (32); jump stop (33); stride stop (34); chest pass (38); bounce pass (38); interception stance (44, 98); V-cut (47); back-door cut (48); pump fake (75); pump-fake crossover (75); fence slide (96); front foot to pivot foot (97); advance step (99); retreat step (99); swing step (99); jump to the ball (103); flash pivot defense (105); dribbler closeout (106); skip pass and closeout (107)

Advanced

1. Line up as shown in figure 1. Rotate from 1 to X1 to the end of the line.

2. This is an eight-part drill: four strong side (figure 1) and four weak side (figure 2). You may drill on all eight points in one day, or strong side one day and weak side the next.

3. Player 1 passes to the coach. X1 must jump to the ball (part 1). This compels 1 to go back-door. He stops in the post and X1 plays post defense (part 2). If the coach can pass to 1, 1 and X1 go one-on-one inside. If so, 1 and X1 return to the low post to continue the eight-part drill. Player 1 breaks out to the corner, and X1 denies the corner (part 3); 1 can break back-door if X1 makes it available. Anywhere 1 gets the ball, he squares up in triple-threat position and the two players go one-on-one (part 4). This makes up the strong-side four.

4. After drilling on the strong side, or when 1 initially cuts, the two end up again at the low post. From here, 1 breaks to the weak side, and the weak-side four begins. Player 1 may move up and down the sideline, inbounds only about three feet, to keep X1's coverage honest. First X1 must get in interception stance position (part 1). X1 must be two-thirds the distance from the coach and one-third the distance from 1. He also must be one step off the line between 1 and the ball (coach). The coach rolls the ball hard toward 1, and X1 must pivot and intercept this pass. X1 gives the ball back to the coach, and the coach begins a drive baseline or middle. X1 must close out on the breakaway dribbler (part 2). Then the coach tosses a lob pass over to 1, and X1 must close out on the pass receiver (part 3). Player 1 squares up in triple-threat position, and the two play one-on-one. After this, the ball is tossed back to the coach, and 1 flash pivots. X1 must deny this flash pivot cut (part 4); 1 can go back-door if X1 makes it available. When 1 gets the ball, X1 and 1 play one-on-one.

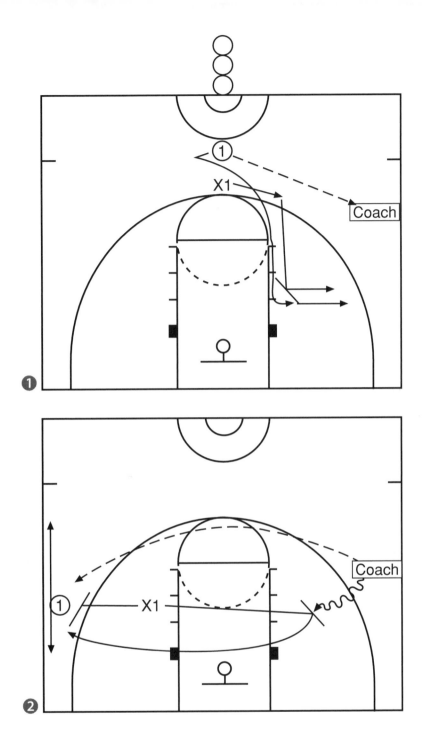

Related Drills: 6, 8-12, 24-27, 31-34, 38, 47, 49, 75, 96, 97, 99-101, 104, 106, 107, 109, 110

CHAPTER 17

Team Defense

Your team defense will never be stronger than the weakest individual playing it. That's why you want to spend an inordinate amount of time developing the individual. Stance is most important. Hence, all players must be adept at the fence slide (drill 96). Without front foot to pivot foot stance (drill 97), you can never dictate to your assignment where you will allow him to go. Then there are the weak-side and interception stances (drill 98). Don't go to footwork until stance is mastered.

Now the attacker will be using moves on you, including dribbling drives. Hence, you need the advance step, retreat step, swing step, and the slide step (all in drill 99). This should allow you to stop the first few dribbles. But you want to dominate and dictate even in drives you will allow. Hence, you need the overplay step (drill 100).

Now you are in proper position. You are ready to help your teammates. Your rules:

1. Jump to the ball (drill 103)
2. Deny the wing (drill 104)
3. Deny the flash pivot (drill 105)
4. Close out to the dribbler (drill 106)—this requires a team rotation, given in the Shell Drill (drill 109)
5. Close out to the pass receiver (drill 107)

The Shell Drill, drill 109, is broken into 10 different parts. You may drill each separately, or you may allow random movement by the four attackers, and the defenders must react to those choices. Then you need to drill five-on-five (drill 110), activating the individual techniques and tactics, the five rules previously mentioned, and the rotation drill discussed in drill 109.

109 Shell Drill

Team • 10 minutes

Skill Focus ▶ Triple-threat position (6); rocker step (8); in and out (9, 24); crossover (10, 25); spin (11, 26); half spin (12, 27); front pivot (31); reverse pivot (32); jump stop (33); stride stop (34); chest pass (38); bounce pass (38); interception stance (44, 98); V-cut (47); middle cut (48); back-door cut (49); pump fake (75); pump-fake crossover (75); fence slide (96); front foot to pivot foot (97); advance step (99); retreat step (99); swing step (99); jump to the ball (103); flash pivot defense (105); dribbler closeout (106); skip pass and closeout (107); rotation

Advanced

1. Line players up in any formation, four attackers and four defenders. You should change formations from day to day: choose among 2-2, 1-3, 1-2-1, and so on. You may wish to drill against your next opponent's formation. After two minutes or so, rotate 1 and 2 and X1 and X2 to play 3 and 4 and X3 and X4's positions. This permits all players to play defense on guards and on wings (corners). Rotate from offense to defense after five minutes, or require the defense to stop the attackers two straight times before rotating.

2. The only new thing to learn is the rotation. Figure 1 illustrates the drive of the baseline; and figure 2 illustrates a typical drive to the inside. Both are defended using the same defensive rules: Weak-side deep defender, X4, yells "rotate" and picks up the breakaway dribbler. Weak-side outside defender, X2, drops to defend the basket. The defender on the breakaway dribbler rotates to cover the open attacker. X3 should have denied the pass to 3 in figure 1. And X2 should have closed the gap on the dribbler in figure 2. Both were defensive mistakes that occurred before the dribbler penetrated. Then both defenders on the ball did not have their players under control, dictating and dominating, before the penetrating dribble. But that is what basketball is: a series of mistakes, some compelled by excellent fakes, some because of lack of concentration. That is the purpose of the rotation tactic. It allows the defense one last chance to stop the ball and correct a previous defensive mistake.

3. *Positioning:* 1, 2, 3, and 4 pass the ball around, using skip passes if they wish. Each player holds the ball three seconds while drilling on this phase separately. X1, X2, X3, and X4 jump to the ball while the pass is in flight.

4. *Close the gap:* 1, 2, 3, and 4 takes turns dribbling toward the basket. X1, X2, X3, and X4 must help on this drive and then recover to their own assignments. The closest defender on the drive side should step in, preventing the further penetration by the dribbler. If the defender is in proper jump to the ball position, it is easy to accomplish.

5. *Pass penetration:* Whenever a pass is completed into a side, high, or low post, the perimeter defender nearest the pass receiver must dive into the area of the ball, forcing the pass back out to the perimeter.

6. *Flash pivot defense:* Player 1 passes to 3; 4 flash pivots. X3 should have denied the penetrating pass to 3. But now X4 must deny the flash pivot pass to 4. X2 and X1 sag to help X4 on 4. X4 and 4 play one-on-one until the pass comes back out to the perimeter.

7. *Cutter drill:* Whenever a pass is made, the passer cuts to another position. His defender must jump to the ball: middle cuts must never be allowed. Other attackers V-cut to keep 15-foot spacing.

8. *Screen away:* Any player who passes goes to screen away. The two players involved in the screen away can run the screen and roll, the screen and fade, or the screen and replace. The passer must read the defense's tactics: Do they switch? Do they stay with their assignment? This tells the passer the primary target and the secondary target.

9. *Screen on ball:* Any player passing to a teammate can go screen for that teammate. They may screen and roll, screen and fade, screen and replace. Defenders away from the ball should be jumping to the ball. These defenders should sag even farther to help on the screening maneuvers.

10. *Shell drill with a post:* Activate your post defense. Do you want to cover three-quarters? Do you want to front? Do you want to play behind the post? Whenever a pass goes into the post, all perimeter defenders should dive toward the ball to help the post defender.

11. *Two or more tactics:* The beauty of this drill is that you can create any combination of defensive techniques and tactics you wish to work on. For example, you are going to work only on parts 4 and 7 today. That means you are going to allow dribblers to penetrate as far as they can, and you are going to permit cutting on every pass. This use of combinations allows you to work on what gave you trouble in the last game. You may even use three parts at one time.

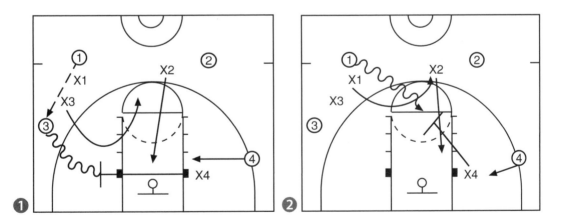

Related Drills: 6, 8-12, 24-27, 31-34, 38, 47, 49, 75, 96, 97, 99-101, 104, 106-108, 110

110 Five-on-Five

Team • As long as needed

Skill Focus ▷ Practice all learned skills; motion offense rules; defensive team rules

1. Line up in some type of formation. Change this formation from day to day. Go over the motion offense rules and the defensive team rules. Limit the rules in accordance with your talent. If your players can only handle three offensive rules, then use only three. Same for the defensive rules.
2. Offense and defense switch roles after each score.

Options ▷
1. Defense must stop the offense a certain number of consecutive possessions before teams switch roles.
2. Give the offense 10 possessions. Keep track of how many times they scored. Now rotate and give the new offense 10 possessions. The team that scored the most, wins.
3. Limit the way the offense can score. You may use several techniques and tactics, such as cutting, dribbling, and screening on the ball. But once a few techniques are designated, allow nothing else.
4. Tell the offense only a certain player can score. You will notice how hard screens are set to free that individual instead of just one-on-one play.
5. Tell the offense the only score allowed is anything shot within five feet. Notice how hard players work to pass penetrate, dribble penetrate, and rebound.

Related Drills: All

Appendix: Organizing Practice Sessions

Before you begin the season, decide which parts of the motion offense you wish to run. This should be determined by your players. How old are they? How experienced are they? What type of athletes do you have? The answers to these questions should help you establish how many rules your motion offense will have. A minimum of two rules will do: that allows your players to play one-on-one. Then you might add the cutting maneuvers. Then, as the season progresses and your players improve, you might add the screening maneuvers.

Next you must resolve how much of the man-to-man defense you want to teach. Ask the same questions. You may simply develop the one-on-one stances, footwork, and slides, and leave it at that. Or you may want to add weak-side defensive help. Or maybe even get into trapping as the season progresses and your players improve.

Once these two major tenets are decided, you are ready to consider the drills you are going to use. You need to establish certain rules of practice so your practices will be well organized and zippy. Kids do not like to stand around. They learn best by doing and being active.

The drills will allow your players to be active, to learn, and to improve. The book concludes with a discussion on running a successful practice and on organizing your drills to maximize your practice time.

How to Run a Successful Practice

First, sit down before the practice season begins and determine how much practice time you are allotted before your first game. This will establish which drills you can spend more time on and which will have to be relegated to smaller portions of time.

Have this as your squad's first rule: Whenever you hear a whistle, you stop what you are doing and meet (or stay) at a predetermined spot. We always liked for our players to stay just where they were. Several drills could be run from that spot before taking up a new sequence of drills. But if they heard two whistles—one after another—then they were to meet at a predetermined basket at the end of the court. We used this area to explain our next set of drills.

Have this as a second rule: Absolutely no talking.

You are now ready to begin practicing. It is that simple.

Have a written daily practice plan. If you are a youth league coach and can get several moms or dads to help you, you will have many on-the-floor "assistant" coaches. You might do all the explaining of the drills, but your assistants can help supervise. Give each member of your "coaching staff" a copy of the daily practice plan.

If you are a middle school or high school coach, you probably have paid assistant coaches. But if you know of a sandlot coach who has used this book to teach, you would be wise to "add" them to your staff. You can break down your numbers and get more repetitions in any drill with more coaches.

Have a method of keeping up with your weekly practices and your monthly practices by checking off each fundamental on an all-inclusive board at home. This eliminates leaving out any portion of the game. You can see immediately if something important has been omitted during the week or the month. And you can include a drill that teaches that concept in your next daily practice plan. The 17 different chapter titles in the table of contents can form your list.

Now you are ready to begin drilling those eager youngsters. And what's more, they will get the maximum training from their practice time. You are organized. You are armed with knowledge (this book will give you that). And you are enthused. Yes. Yes. Yes. You must be enthusiastic. It is contagious, like a common cold.

You want each drill to be short. We have kept each to a level of no more than 10 minutes. Most are less. Young minds begin to wander if held to one task too long. You can change to a related drill (each drill in this book is shown with related drills) and get the same fundamental covered and stop boring your players. Or you can change to an entirely different fundamental and come back to the former essential at a later spot in your practice schedule.

You want as few players in each drill as possible. This allows more repetitions under supervision. The more repetitions, the more the muscle memory develops, and the sooner the player begins to perform the fundamental accurately and quickly. And the kids will appreciate this. That is why we said earlier: get several moms and dads to agree to be assistants.

Make each drill fun and competitive. We have done this in each drill. Just follow the procedures. But keep in mind: some of the drills naturally lean toward more learning and some of them toward more fun. You can tell by the feel of the group whether you need more learning or more fun. A good rule to follow: Do a fun drill after every two learning drills. Then when you start winning and winning and winning, you will find winning has its own form of fun, making learning drills more enjoyable.

Explain every drill in detail. Just follow the teaching points and the procedure. You want to emphasize only one or two teaching points each drill. The player will remember few points more readily than many.

Demonstrate every technique that will be taught in that drill. We have held many drills to one technique. If you cannot demonstrate, get an assistant to do so while you explain the drill. There are many "older players" who would be happy to come and demonstrate at your practices.

After explaining and demonstrating, break into your little groups and let the kids perform the drill. You are now ready to supervise. Keep your talking to a minimum. Keep the drilling to a maximum. People learn best by doing.

When game time arrives, you have to deputize. Your players have to play the game. The youngster's performance will display to you what your next practices must include. Each practice and each game should be used to further develop the players. Each practice and game should be used as an ever-expanding improvement session. That's where real success is.

How to Devise a Practice Schedule

There are many questions to consider when building a practice schedule: Is it early, middle, or late season? How much practice time do you have? What are you planning on running teamwise? What did not work well in the last practice or latest game? These are just a few elements you must consider.

There are infinite components to ponder; so many that an entire book can be written just on devising a practice schedule. And to a great degree, the success of your team depends on carefully thought out practice schedules. Sample practice schedules are given in the following pages for 30 minutes and 90 minutes for each of the three major phases of the season—early, middle, and late. From this you can get ideas of how you should develop your practice schedule. Drill numbers are listed, followed by the time it takes to run the drill, and a reason we include the drill. You can use the drill finder on page vi when developing your practice schedule: each drill is listed there along with the time required to run that drill.

30-minute practice—early season		
Drill number	**Time (minutes)**	**Drill activity**
Drill 1	3	Fundamental foot movement and conditioning
Drill 5	3	Shooting layups
Drill 6	2	Triple-threat position
Drill 15	2	Ballhandling
Drill 19	1	Speed dribbling
Drill 24	1	Teaching a move and dribbling
Drill 25	1	Teaching another move and dribbling
Drill 26	1	Ballhandling, move, agility, conditioning
Drill 31	2	Pivoting
Drill 32	2	Pivoting
Drill 33	1	Stopping
Drill 38	3	Passing
Drill 47	3	Cutting
Drill 48	3	Cutting, triple-threat position, and moves

You can see from this practice schedule that you are planning on running your motion offense using cuts and one-on-one play.

30-minute practice—mid-season

Drill number	Time (minutes)	Drill activity
Drill 8	1	Rocker step
Drill 11	1	Spin dribbling move
Drill 12	1	Half-spin move
Drill 26	1	Emphasizing spin move and ballhandling
Drill 27	1	Emphasizing half spin and ballhandling
Drill 26	1	Two-ball variation
Drill 27	1	Two-ball variation
Drill 48	5	Cutting, layups, and moves
Drill 49	3	Back-door cuts
Drill 56	4	Team offensive tactics
Drill 72	10	Shooting

You can see from this practice schedule that you are reviewing two moves and some cutting maneuvers, working on your shots, and running your team offense.

30-minute practice—late season

Drill number	Time (minutes)	Drill activity
Drill 21	1	Ballhandling, warming up, and agility
Drill 28	2	Ballhandling, warming up, and agility
Drill 92	5	Reviewing your offense
Drill 73	6	Shooting
Drill 101	2	Reviewing your individual defense
Drill 109	10	Working on team defense
Drill 110	4	Live offense versus live defense

You can see from this practice session that you are reviewing your offense and defense, improving on shooting, and scrimmaging.

90-minute practice—early season

Drill number	Time (minutes)	Drill activity
Drill 1	3	Footwork, conditioning
Drill 8	1	Footwork
Drill 10	1	Another move
Drill 12	1	Another move
Drill 24	1	Stressing the chosen move, agility, ballhandling
Drill 25	1	Stressing the chosen move, agility, ballhandling
Drill 26	1	Stressing the chosen move, agility, ballhandling
Drill 27	1	Stressing the chosen move, agility, ballhandling

Drill number	Time (minutes)	Drill activity
Drill 32	2	Pivoting
Drill 34	1	Stopping
Drill 40	2	Passing and conditioning
Drill 47	3	V-cut
Drill 48	3	Middle cut
Drill 49	3	Back-door cut
Drill 52	3	Recognition of when to cut
Drill 59	10	Passing, cutting, and screening away
Drill 70	1	Reviewing proper shooting technique
Drill 71	10	Shooting
Drill 100	2	Reviewing individual defense
Drill 101	2	Reviewing individual defense
Drill 83	4	Live one-on-one
Drill 88	6	Hustle, live one-on-one
Drill 103	5	Reviewing phase of individual defense
Drill 105	4	Reviewing another phase of individual defense
Drill 107	6	Live one-on-one after reviewing closing out

You can see from this practice schedule that you have had a few prior workouts, but it is still early in the season. You are planning on your motion offense including one-on-one play, cutting, and screening. And you intend to be really good defensively because of your stress on defensive drills.

90-minute practice—mid-season		
Drill number	Time (minutes)	Drill activity
Drill 4	1	Conditioning and defensive footwork
Drill 6	2	Offensive stance
Drill 8	1	Offensive footwork before the dribble
Drill 24	1	Conditioning, ballhandling, and footwork
Drill 25	1	Conditioning, ballhandling, and footwork
Drill 26	1	Conditioning, ballhandling, and footwork
Drill 27	1	Conditioning, ballhandling, and footwork
Drill 35	$1\frac{1}{2}$	Protection of the ball
Drill 44	10	Protection of the ball and trapping
Drill 51	10	Offensive footwork
Drill 57	6	Review cutting, footwork, dribbling, and defense
Drill 108	10	Individual/team defensive fundamentals
Drill 72	10	Shooting
Drill 91	10	Review your motion offense
Drill 109	10	Review your team defense
Drill 110	14	Scrimmage

You can see from this practice schedule that you had turnover trouble in your last game, so you work to improve that. You also want to work on your fundamental offensive and defensive footwork. And at the end you want to see if that improvement was evident in scrimmage situations.

90-minute practice—late season		
Drill number	**Time (minutes)**	**Drill activity**
Drill 1	3	Conditioning, agility, and footwork
Drill 13	3	All dribbling moves
Drill 24	1	Conditioning and dribble move
Drill 25	1	Conditioning and dribble move
Drill 26	1	Conditioning and dribble move
Drill 27	1	Conditioning and dribble move
Drill 37	3	Pivoting, stopping, and dribbling
Drill 56	4	Passing, cutting, and spacing: your motion offense
Drill 72	10	Shooting
Drill 73	6	Shooting
Drill 87	5	Conditioning and one-on-one play
Drill 89	6	Hustle and one-on-one play
Drill 94	9	Review your motion offense rules
Drill 102	1	Review defensive movement off the ball
Drill 108	10	Review individual defensive movement off ball
Drill 110	26	Scrimmage

You have had a layoff of more than a week since your last game. You need to get your team back into game condition; and you need to review your offense and your defense. It is still a couple of days until you play again. Hence, you scrimmage more as well as review different parts of your offense and defense. And your shooting was a little rusty. Taper off the scrimmaging in your next two practice sessions and work more on fundamentals. This will not only improve your squad physically but also make them more eager to play the game.

More games are won or lost in practices than on game day. And you can never go wrong if your players are always improving, always learning, always progressing. For them, tomorrow is much more important than today.

About the Authors

Burrall Paye has been developing young basketball players' skills for more than 30 years. He is considered one of the game's best teachers.

Coach Paye enjoyed winning seasons in 36 of the 37 years that he coached. During his career he was honored as State Coach of the Year and National Federation Interscholastic Coaches Association Outstanding Coach (1985).

Now retired, Coach Paye shares his expertise through his speaking and writing. He has spoken at major clinics in the United States, Canada, Mexico, and Europe. His numerous articles have appeared in newspapers and magazines such as *Scholastic Coach, Basketball Clinic, Coaching Clinic, Pro-Keds Digest*, and *Winning Hoops*. He is the author of several books on basketball, including *Playing the Post* (Human Kinetics, 1996).

Paye earned his master's degree in 1965 from the University of Tennessee. He is a member of the National High School Coaches Association and the Virginia High School Coaches Association. He lives in Roanoke, Virginia, with his wife, Nancy.

Burrall's son **Patrick Paye** is a successful coach as well. He is currently the head boys' basketball coach at Northeastern High School in Elizabeth City, North Carolina. Patrick has never been a part of a losing season as a player or coach in a collegiate playing career and 11 years of coaching at the college and high school levels. He has rebuilt two traditionally losing programs into playoff teams during his career as a high school coach. Patrick, his wife, Michele, and their son, Rylan reside in Grandy, North Carolina.